There are many things I could commend about the helpfulness of this book, but what stuck with me is the possibility by God's grace of worshiping Him in everything I do, rather than just getting buried by my to-do list and feeling overwhelmed. As a woman who longs to be organized and have a peaceful and joyful heart, the Scriptures and reminders that Trisha uses take me to my knees asking Jesus for His faithful help.

Do you feel buried by your to-do list, overwhelmed, or lack joy in what you are doing? *Everyday Worship* sheds light on the path that Jesus takes us on as we journey toward worshiping Him in ALL we do. Peace, His love, and joy take the place of our anxious hearts as we repent and let Him guide our schedule daily.

Grace Driscoll
Pastor's daughter, Pastor's wife, Mother of 5
NY Times #1 Best-selling co-author of *Real Marriage*
Seattle, Washington

In *Everyday Worship*, Trisha Wilkerson walks the tightrope of avoiding legalism while talking about grace-motivated work. There is seldom a time where I read about the Proverbs 31 woman without feeling crushing guilt. Trisha was able to walk me through those verses without condemnation. She did this by pointing me to Christ in every chapter of this book. With refreshing honesty and relatable candor she opens up her life in an encouraging way. She renewed in my heart a passion to work as worship for all that Jesus has done for me. This book will be very helpful for those of us who are learning how to work as unto the Lord.

Jessica Thompson
Co-author of *Give Them Grace*
Poway, California

Thank you Trisha. You have reminded us that we are made for worship. These personal insights clothed in a practical and spiritual way are refreshing. This timely book should focus our minds on The Lord Jesus Christ so that we worship God "whatever, whenever, however".

Carine Mackenzie
Best-selling author of children's books
Inverness, Scotland

The honest, inquisitive, Jesus-loving voice you read in this book is the same voice that Trisha speaks into the lives of her family, friends and counselees. As a long-time friend, I can assure you her life reflects her writing – with the truth and tenderness of one who has been transformed by Jesus. She invites all women to experience the freedom and joy that work and worship can bring when Jesus is the center. Pick up this book and learn from her wisdom.

Jennifer Smidt
Blogger, www.theresurgence.com
Seattle, Washington

As Christian women we search for balance in the mundane and chaos of life. *Everyday Worship* addresses the heart battles that keep us from worshiping Jesus throughout the day.

Trisha examines the many facets of life that every woman faces, then draws you back to the gospel through her heart-probing questions at the end of each chapter.

Regardless of whether you work in or outside of your home, I highly recommend you get a cup of coffee and begin reading *Everyday Worship* so that you can experience God's grace and love more deeply in your everyday life.

Karen Cheong
Pastor's wife and Ministry leader, Sojourn Community Church
Louisville, Kentucky

When the theme of godly work and ambition is brought up, we tend to either perk up from pride or we breathe the deep sigh of failure and guilt. In her book, *Everyday Worship*, Trisha Wilkerson invites women to understand how our work can be redeemed through its vital connection to the invigorating stream of worship. Biblically-saturated, refreshingly honest, and practically helpful, this book is a gift of encouragement and inspiration to women like myself who want to work heartily while being motivated and sustained by the life-giving grace of Christ.

Keri Seavey
Pastor's wife and Biblical counselor
Living Water Community Church, Vancouver, Washington

Like many women, I struggle to connect my work to worship. I often catch myself striving for value, significance and approval from my work and those with whom I work. Trisha Wilkerson reminds us that whenever we do that we lose sight of our loving Father who is already pleased with us because of Jesus. Her book was a great reminder to me that all of my work, at the end of the day, is meaningless apart from Christ. Read this book and be encouraged yourself to live a whole, authentic life where your work *is* worship.

Karen Jacklin Teears
President, New Growth Press
Greensboro, North Carolina

Too often in my own life, my heart is disconnected from God as I go about my daily tasks. I can be task-oriented, work-resistant, and/or convenience-seeking rather than Christ-oriented, Holy Spirit-dependent, and God's glory-seeking. This devotional book offers plenty of heart-checks to assess not only the work that we do, but also our motivations and aims as we go about our work.

I'll admit. I don't often worship in the midst of my work. My work looks and feels like a pile of never-ending tasks. Trisha has helped me to see that those piles are actually opportunities to worship the Lord of glory who calls us to do everything in humility, without complaining, and heartily as unto the Lord, in dependence upon Him to accomplish His work in and through me.

I recommend this book for any like me who desire to have a heart of worship in the midst of our daily responsibilities, and who need a fresh reminder to worship the Lord in every area and circumstance of life.

Kristie Anyabwile
Pastor's wife, Mother of 3
Grand Cayman, Cayman Islands

Everyday Worship

Our Work, Heart and Jesus

TRISHA WILKERSON

CHRISTIAN
FOCUS

Trisha Wilkerson is a blogger for The Resurgence, and a biblical counselor and women's leader at Mars Hill Church. She is the wife of Pastor Mike Wilkerson who oversees Redemption Groups at Mars Hill. They are the parents of four young children and make their home in Seattle, Washington.

Copyright © Trisha Wilkerson 2013
paperback ISBN 978-1-78191-155-6
epub ISBN 978-1-78191-263-8
Mobi ISBN 978-1-78191-264-5

10 9 8 7 6 5 4 3 2 1

Published in 2013
by
Christian Focus Publications Ltd,
Geanies House, Fearn,
Ross-shire, IV20 1TW, Scotland.
www.christianfocus.com

Cover design
by
Daniel van Straaten

Printed by
Bell and Bain, Glasgow

MIX
Paper from
responsible sources
FSC
www.fsc.org
FSC® C007785

CONTENTS

Introduction: The War of Work and Worship 11

PART ONE: Choosing the Good Portion

1 Is Mary Greater Than Martha? 19
2 Jesus is the Good Portion 25
3 Who Do We Work For? 31
4 Ambition: Selfish or Godly? 41
5 From Overwhelmed to Overjoyed 47
6 Less Control, More Worship 53
7 "Heart" Battles: Fighting to Worship 59

PART TWO: A Woman Who Fears the Lord

8 Imitate, Don't Idolize 67
9 Jesus is Greater Than the Proverbs 31 Woman....71
10 Fear of the Lord 77
11 Works With Willing Hands 83
12 Meekness: True Strength 91
13 Mission Minded 97
14 Wise, Worshipful Words 103

PART THREE: Worship: Our Response to Jesus

15 We Need a Gospel Vision 113
16 We Are His Workmanship 121
17 Prayer Brings Peace 129
18 Rest for the Weary 137

PART FOUR: Heart Change

19 From Busy-Body to Busy Bee 145
20 From Sluggard to Steward 153
21 From Independence to Dependence 161

22 From Grumbling to Gratitude 167

23 From Isolation to Community 173

PART FIVE: A Woman's Home

24 A Beautiful Heart, A Beautiful Home 183

25 Practicing Biblical Hospitality 191

26 Productive Planning 199

PART SIX: Worship Is All About Jesus

27 Getting and Giving Grace 207

28 Invitation to Worship 215

To my husband, Michael –
my best friend and daily partner in the gospel.

Introduction:

The War
of
Work and Worship

There is a battle raging in our hearts: a war of work and worship. Worship recognizes God's holiness and reflects that holiness in our daily lives, while depending entirely upon God's grace. Work, too often, is just work—when our hearts are disconnected from God in what we're doing. Our vision becomes nearsighted, clouded by our daily task lists. When we do try to bring God into our daily lives, He ends up on the task list, usually at the bottom. We find ourselves overwhelmed and burdened by the demands, missing out on God while we rush through our work. At the end of the day, we may thank God for the accomplishments, yet feel dissatisfied and disconnected from Him.

Over the last few years I've noticed something in myself and others: sometimes working hard feels good, but most of the time, it leaves us empty and unsatisfied. The rush of standing back to observe the "before and after" soon wanes. An orderly room doesn't feel as good as it used to.

When I talk about work in this book, this includes a broad spectrum of work. From a stay-at-home mom with young children to a suit-wearing career woman, we all work. We all get up in the morning and do something. Office job or home job, we all labor and have various heart experiences in light of what God has called us to do. We are all working women.

For me, I am a stay-at-home momma, so my personal references will be mostly about the home and family. My prayer is that, whatever season of life you are in, you will be able to relate to the work and worship struggle discussed in these chapters.

A confession: I have dutifully worked without worshiping God. Working hard with my own willpower, work ethic, and independent desire to get results has allowed me to feel the satisfaction of the end product instead of being satisfied in Christ throughout my days. I've had godless ambition and gotten angry at anyone who stood in the way of getting work done, which stole the sweetness of knowing God in my work. The drive to accomplish has enticed me far more than the enjoyment of God's presence.

The independent streak in my heart rebelled at the thought of acknowledging God's hand in my work! Depend on Jesus with the mundane tasks of life? "You're kidding," I'd say to God. But God wasn't kidding. He led me through various life lessons, teaching me to depend on Him in my work, and I'm sure He will continue.

God gently invited me to see my arrogant work ethic, patiently revealing my need for forgiveness. He softened my heart, melting my icy self-sufficiency. Exposed and wrecked, I began to see my sin and how blind I had been. I started feeling grief for my vain work that I had baptized with Christian phrases, sometimes offering half-hearted thanks to God at the end of my productivity, but not being mindful of Jesus throughout my day. My vision was laser-focused on tasks, not on Jesus.

Over time, I replaced thoughts of my Savior with a drive to accomplish my tasks. My once-aggressive, obsessively organized self has gradually, and remarkably, begun to tenderly depend on God in the details of my day. When I was a new mother, tenderness and dependence on God started replacing a numb and dutiful work ethic. My daily tasks took on new meaning. With fresh repentance, the Holy Spirit challenged me to journey into Scripture to seek what God had to say about me as a woman concerning my calling, worship, and work.

The journey has been exciting! Thankfully, God is faithful to reveal Himself as I have submitted to Him in the details of my daily work. My hands are still feverishly working. Change has been slow, and continues. But I am more able to see my sin of idolatrous work, and my work has begun to reflect His grace.

Through leading women's Bible studies, coaching leaders, and counseling women in our church, I have seen women's hearts up close and discovered I am not alone. I am surrounded by countless women who live in the whirlwind of duty-driven, stressed-out, godless effort.

The challenge of connecting work to worship is as old as the story of Martha and Mary in Luke 10. Women struggle between two extremes: from feminist ideas of our identity found in work, to the sloth with no ambition who scorns goals. Tragically, each of these extremes involves a distortion in our view of God. When we strive for value, significance, and approval in the eyes of our bosses, parents or anyone else who will praise our work, we lose sight of our loving Father who is already pleased because of His Son. When we swing to the slothful extreme and reject hard work or settle for half-hearted vision, we miss out on God's holy purpose for our lives. All of this work, at the end of the day— meaningless effort, apart from Jesus.

What About You?

So, why should you read this? Why should you hear the details of my struggle, sin, and repentance? It is my hope and intention to challenge and inspire you to look deep into your heart and allow God to help you change.

I believe we all are rebellious and resist dependence on God in some category of our lives. Perhaps you picked this book up by God's providence, in need of Jesus opening your eyes to see your misplaced worship and to be changed by Him.

If we were at coffee together, I would ask you several questions. Please consider them and journal your thoughts. Pray for a soft heart and clarity along the way.

1. What are your work struggles?

2. When does work frustrate you?

3. Do you see yourself more as lazy or ambitious?

4. When do you feel anxious or stressed out about your home or work?

5. What gets in the way of completing your work?

6. Are you aware of God when you work?

7. What are you thinking or feeling when you are working?

8. Are you aware of where your heart is tempted when you are overwhelmed?

9. Do you see work as worship?

Are You an Overachiever or Overwhelmed?

Do you identify with the Overachiever or the Overwhelmed? Depending on the season I am in, I may feel like I am on top of my work, getting it all done. Or, I may feel completely overwhelmed. The Overachiever tends to struggle with self-sufficiency and independence from God. This happens when we think that we can do our work without God's help. The Overwhelmed tends to struggle with apathy and sluggard tendencies. Both, though, reveal a deep need for God's grace to shine a light on our lack of dependence on God.

Maybe you find yourself on the apathetic or idle side of the work and worship spectrum. As a mom, maybe you lack vision, direction, and intentionality. You struggle to know which method is wisest, you compare yourself to other moms and their methods, and you often feel condemned, like you never measure up. Envy and insecurity color your relationship to work in your home and your family. You can't relate to the overachiever who has extra time to take a nap—you can't even find your bed!

Perhaps you are working your 9–5 job and you hate it. You would give anything to leave your job and do something that you love instead. You work hard, but your heart isn't in it. Or you have a great job, and you aren't grateful for it. You are simply apathetic, grumbling in your work. You complain, because your work is beneath you.

We all work and we all have responses to work. Responses that reveal heart motivations. Responses that tell us something about our belief in God.

Your response to your work isn't *who you are*. Wherever you find yourself on this spectrum, you might be tempted to take on your tendencies as your identity: lazy, undisciplined, procrastinating, busy, efficient, accomplished. Seeing your tendencies is helpful, so long as the introspection leads you to Jesus. Your tendencies are not who you are. Rejecting these false identities is an essential part of our worship.

An Invitation

Rather than placing guilt on women with the "should's" of awesome biblical womanhood, this book addresses the heart issues underlying why we often relegate God to the "spiritual" categories of our lives, and how, instead, we can worship Him daily in our work. When we see Jesus in everything from the significant to the mundane, worship is our response, and we start beholding Him as He is. Our vision begins to clear as we see Christ in our common duties and we see Him *with* us, loving us, and deserving of our gratitude—our humble worship.

You might feel like you're ready for a practical list of things to do to start worshiping better in your work. If I gave you that list right now, you might apply and improve a little, but soon, your motivation would wane. Lasting change in behavior requires deep change in the heart. Deep change in the heart means a change of worship. Worship starts with God.

So, throughout the book, we will learn to see Him differently. We must rest in knowing God as the Master Worker who gives us Himself, sanctifies us by His grace, and calls us to work that reveals our continual need for Him. Worship is the overflow of our hearts, which are thankful for His steadfast love and constant help. Our reward at the end of the day's work? Jesus Himself. God is with us and will be with us. That promise convicts and compels us to worship in our work.

This is not a legalistic "how to" manual for Christian womanhood, but a grace-saturated charge for women to see all of life as worship and savor Jesus as the reason for our worship. Our work is not about us; it is an opportunity to worship Jesus!

Would you join me in exploring the possibility of worship in your work?

PART ONE:

Choosing
the Good Portion

CHAPTER 1

Is Mary Greater
than Martha?

Martha. Martha. Martha.

Some of us are very familiar with the story of the two famous sisters in Luke 10. Whether this story is familiar or fresh for you, I'm convinced there is revolutionary heart change available in the depth of this story. One reason God chose to include this particular event is for us to learn more about the common heart battle with work and worship.

> Now as they went on their way, Jesus entered a village. And a woman named Martha welcomed him into her house. And she had a sister called Mary, who sat at the Lord's feet and listened to his teaching. But Martha was distracted with much serving. And she went up to him and said, "Lord, do you not care that my sister has left me to serve alone? Tell her then to help me." But the Lord answered her, "Martha, Martha, you are anxious and troubled about many things, but one thing is necessary. Mary has chosen the good portion, which will not be taken away from her." (Luke 10:38-42)

Mary made a good choice; she chose worship.

Let me offer a warning: Resist the temptation to see yourself as either Martha or Mary. While it is natural to connect with these characters, this story is not about how some personality types lead to worship while others don't. If we're encouraged to be more like Mary than Martha in this story, it's not because we all need to have Mary's personality type—more relational—but because she set a good example of worship. Martha could have worshiped too, despite being more attentive to tasks.

Mary's personality trait here is often exalted as the holy one, the "relational gal" who sits at Jesus' feet learning, listening, and loving. But Jesus wasn't attaching worth to a personality, and neither should we. Our focus and His is *worship*. We will get to Mary in the next chapter, but for now, let's explore Martha's struggle.

MARTHA IS TYPE A

All of my Christian life, I heard about the differences between Martha and Mary. Often it was suggested that Martha is the stressed-out sister overly concerned with her tasks. She can't relax because "there is much to be done." Martha works hard but seems to lack the peaceful worship that goes with working heartily unto the Lord. When God Himself is a guest in her home, she can't handle the pressure. She performs tasks while sneering in her sister's direction, complaining that she is bearing the burden alone.

MARTHA IS DISTRACTED

Martha is distracted, but distracted from what? Why is Martha, or anyone, distracted? We think what we're doing is most important: the tasks and preparations. We are focused on the wrong thing. Jesus told Martha she was anxious and troubled about many things. What was she troubled about? Well, I can answer for myself. When I am like Martha—when I am not worshiping in work but just working—I am busy, frustrated, fast, and resentful. My heart's aim is to accomplish, but I work with subtle disdain. Troubled by my work, I resent it if my husband is in the room and not helping in some way. My heart is anxious about the tasks yet-to-be-done. I'm angry that I have to do it all. Maybe I'm trying to enjoy the preparations, but inside my heart, I'm looking for any opportunity to complain that I am going it alone. Distraction is frenzied (either loud or quiet), misplaced worship. I can only assume this was the familiar heart battle for busy Martha.

MARTHA IS A TATTLE-TALE

My kids tattle-tale all the time. They get frustrated and sin in their anger with their siblings because of some apparent offense. The tattler just wants his way. Can't you just picture Martha quietly and busily working, yet raging in her heart? Her anger got the best of her. She wanted Mary to help her! Mary just sat there (!) and listened to Jesus. Martha may have truly started out with a pure heart. She may have had a desire to be hospitable to the Lord, make Him food, and serve Him. So when did her desire to serve turn to sin?

I do the same thing. I tattle-tale in my heart. I complain to God about the people in my house that take me from what I think are more important things: the tasks. Martha complained to the Lord in the flesh. But I do it too—in my heart. I have the same divided heart; tattle-taling while thinking that I am serving.

WHICH GOD ARE WE SERVING?

Again, imagine yourself...imagine me. I am working in the kitchen. I start preparing, and my heart is delighted that I have all the ingredients to make a delicious dinner for my family. I am chopping and peaceful. My husband walks in and greets me and the children. My kids start getting loud in the other room. I stop cooking and attend to their arguments. Then the baby cries. She needs to be comforted. The preparations for this amazing dinner have to stop.

Enter my depravity.

The chaos in the room has threatened my agenda, my peace. Why can't I just get my task done? Why do these kids need me too? Oh, but I love my children...Why does it take so long to make a dinner? I wish I could just focus. Another riot breaks out among the other children and my husband deals with it. Whew! Ok, back to busy preparations. I turn on some music to lighten the attitude in the air, denying the war in my heart. The kids start dancing in the kitchen. I take a break to dance too. They see this opportunity to ask me for a snack. A snack? What? I am making dinner, just be patient! If I could just finish it, they would be happy! I would be happy! I go back to cooking with my heart racing, and my thoughts turn from what started as joyful service to feeling like a martyr.

The war that was raging in me suggests that the god I am serving is The God of Accomplishment and Tasks. I am worshiping the God of Self: *me*.

Martha was worshiping *herself*, not Jesus.

She welcomed Jesus. Perhaps she cheerfully opened the door and showed Him in. At some point, Martha transferred her worship from Jesus to herself. God was actually in her *living room*. She could've sat beside her sister and worshiped Jesus, yet she chose to pursue her own agenda, not God's. She thought serving busily was the right thing to do. She resented her sister as she prepared food for her guests.

The easy and false remedy for this heart struggle would be simple behavior modification: Abandon tasks. Enjoy relationship. Just throw preparations and work out the door and let the good times roll! Play, play, play. Tasks, bad; relationship, good. Martha could've just served crackers and instead joined her sister. Martha, who was concerned with preparations, made a bad choice, and Mary, the relational gal, made the right choice.

Sadly, well-meaning Christians read this story as if it were a fable. Some of these observations are valid. However, Jesus didn't say that doing preparations was wrong. He said Martha was troubled while she did preparations. She could've been doing work humbly and joyfully. Instead, she worked begrudgingly.

MARTHA, REDEEMED

The story could've been:

> Martha was busy with many preparations as she listened to the Lord. In her heart she worshiped Him for enabling her to

enjoy her work as an act of service to Him. Martha offered the fruit of her work in her heart and the Lord ate and was satisfied. Even as Mary sat at the Lord's feet, Martha was not jealous of her sister's behavior, but grateful to have this opportunity to serve the Lord Christ. She worshiped with her hands, with her heart.

We don't know if Martha had another chance to serve Jesus in her home. But, we can assume that she did continue in hospitality. She probably was tempted with sinful thoughts, anxiety, and envy in her heart again. Hopefully, after Jesus corrected her so lovingly, she repented and experienced some redemption with work.

But God saw fit to include another story: Martha's heart battle with work. It is my battle too. But as God changes our hearts, we can worship Jesus in our work.

REFLECTION QUESTIONS

1. When you are busy serving, are you aware of your desires?

2. When do those desires lead you from joyful service to anger or complaining?

3. Would you serve those in your home differently if Jesus were also a guest?

CHAPTER 2

Jesus is
the Good Portion

When we think about Mary as the calm, God-focused worshiper and Martha as the nervous workaholic, we miss the big idea—Jesus. Both women could have worshiped Jesus in their hearts with behavior unique to them. Rather than exalting Mary over Martha, we can explore what was going on in the hearts of both women.

MARY CHOSE THE GOOD PORTION

Mary sat at Jesus' feet and listened to His teaching. When Martha complained, Jesus said, "Mary has chosen the good portion and it will not be taken away from her" (Luke 10:42). Jesus defended Mary and her heart's choice. The good portion was not just that Mary behaved more relationally, sitting and listening, and Martha wasn't rebuked just because she was busy in the kitchen.

Two "meals" were being served: one by Martha and one by Jesus. Mary chose the meal served by Jesus, the better portion, the teaching of God's Word. Her attention was focused on Jesus. Martha's attention was focused on her own preparations. Outwardly, it might have seemed that Martha's attention was on Jesus—she was preparing a meal in His honor after all, wasn't she?

The problem for Martha was not just the preparations, but the focus of her heart. While Martha outwardly seemed to be busy serving Jesus, inwardly her attention was divided. Surely she could have chosen the good portion too, working diligently, with Jesus as her true focus, delighted that Mary's focus was on Jesus too.

When we worship Jesus in our hearts, in whatever we are doing, we choose "the good portion."

MARY IS FLEXIBLE

Martha and Mary lived and worked in the same home in Bethany. They were hospitable and loved Jesus. When Jesus entered their home on the spur of the moment, Mary chose to listen to His teaching, sitting at His feet. She was blessed in this act of worship. It wasn't that sitting at His feet was the best way to worship Jesus; it was in her heart to surrender to worship and cease doing whatever it was she had been doing prior to His arrival. She willingly engaged and seemed to peacefully respond to His presence.

MARY RESPONDS WITH PASSION

In John 11, we read about Lazarus, the brother of Martha and Mary, dying after an illness. Martha left to find Jesus to tell Him the news, and He started walking toward Bethany (Jerusalem, where He was coming from, was just two miles away). When Martha came back to tell Mary that Jesus was asking for her, she jumped up and ran out to meet Him on the road. The Jewish crowd that was with Martha and Mary while they were mourning was so intrigued by Mary's eagerness for Jesus that they went too. When they all got to Jesus, Mary fell at His feet. Her grief moved Him to tears. Jesus, the God of resurrection, could have strolled in to Bethany and calmly raised dead Lazarus to life to prove His power. Instead, He came near to the sisters, showing His humility and care for His friends by comforting and crying with them. Mourner first, Conqueror of Death second. He raised Lazarus as an act of love and a testimony of His own future resurrection (John 11:25). This inspires me as I walk with hurting people. Flying a victory banner over someone's pain doesn't communicate tender love—better to weep with them and remind them of God's affection through patient and humble connection to their experience. Jesus warmly responded to Mary's passion. His love was evident in His tears. He responded perfectly to passion and pain.

MARY IS GENEROUS

In John 12, Mary anoints Jesus with very expensive perfume. Her devoted sister faithfully serves a meal with Jesus as the honored guest in the home of Simon the Leper. Joining them was Lazarus, whom Jesus had just brought back to life, and the disciples. Mary poured this perfume on Jesus' head and feet, then wiped His feet with her hair. Instead of selling this perfume and giving the money to the poor, she chose to worship by anointing her God before His death. Jesus defended her actions, making sure that those who complained about what she had done knew that she was making the good choice, by choosing the good portion.

MARY IS HUMBLE

Wiping Jesus' feet with her hair was truly an act of worship with humility and devotion. I can't imagine doing this. I hope that I would have ignored all of those people around and humbly worshiped my God. I am sad to say my struggle is caring too much what those near would think of me. Mary didn't seem to care. She worshiped Jesus with a passionate decisiveness that I am longing to see lived out in my heart and life!

Psalm 25 comes to mind when I pray for a heart to worship with passion and humility.

> Make me to know your ways, O LORD; teach me your paths. Lead me in your truth and teach me, for you are the God of my salvation; for you I wait all the day long. Remember your mercy, O LORD, and your steadfast love, for they have been from of old. Remember not the sins of my youth or my transgressions; according to your steadfast love remember me, for the sake of your goodness, O LORD! Good and upright is the LORD; therefore he instructs sinners in the way. He leads the

humble in what is right, and teaches the humble his way. All the paths of the LORD are steadfast love and faithfulness, for those who keep his covenant and his testimonies. (Ps. 25:4-10)

CHOOSING THE GOOD PORTION

To choose Jesus is to choose the good portion.

Often distracted with much serving, like Martha, I stop worshiping. I can turn inward and am often thinking and doing "work," when I could be choosing Jesus, the Good Portion. In my laser-focus for tasks, my heart loses sight of worship. My body is active and my heart disengaged.

For the last few years, I have been asking God, "What does it look like to choose the good portion in my work? Can my work be worshipful?"

Every day, God gives me opportunities to learn this through motherhood. Distractions, needs from those around me, and simple demands for my attention present me with a choice.

I can *do* my agenda *or* pray for discernment each moment for the "good portion" decision and submit cheerfully to that.

Today after returning home from an errand, I had one hour to clean up, make lunch, get the older three children back to their school work, and put my three year old down for a nap by the time a 1:00 appointment at my house would begin. The clock and the list of things to do met me at the door, and I set out to achieve my goals for the hour. I saw one of my sons go downstairs, visibly distraught from a conflict he had when we were out on errands. My heart sank. Seriously? I thought, *now?* No. I have to clean the kitchen and prepare lunch! I felt frustrated and interrupted. My plan was now competing with my son. Then, redemptive thoughts began to fill my mind. Attending to my son replaced *my* agenda to accomplish *my* tasks. His little heart is more important than getting my stuff done. We ended up talking for forty-five minutes. Loving my boy and prioritizing him by being willing to drop my agenda was "choosing the good portion" today.

How is this choosing Jesus as the good portion? Well, consider what was at stake for me in that moment. If I take time out to serve my son, I may not have the house quite as prepared for my one o'clock guest as I would like. I wanted her to see me as well prepared. But would I trade that impression for a disheartened son? How did Jesus want to minister to both my son and my one o'clock guest, and what sacrifice might He have been calling me to make to follow *His* ministry agenda for the afternoon?

My heart is so easily swept away by my desires and plans. While ambition and hard work can be strengths, they can also be a temptation to prioritize the wrong things.

There are also times where choosing the good portion involves tasks. Martha could relate to this story: One Monday morning, I woke up exhausted. My husband had just returned home from a week of travel. I had spent that week wearily caring for our four children. I was ready to sleep in and let my husband have a turn caring for the children. However, it was our son's birthday. We have a tradition of birthday morning breakfast in bed. Will I get up early and work?

Someone at this point will offer the good advice: *How about your husband makes the breakfast?*

My son was expecting my special pancakes and bacon. The point wasn't how to solve the problem—sure, my husband would've willingly served. It was about my heart: would I lean in to Jesus and choose the good portion? In this case, that would mean doing tasks in love.

Choosing Jesus is an ongoing moment-by-moment dependence on the Holy Spirit.

Reflection Questions

1. Do you see yourself as flexible when your plan is interrupted?

2. What tends to get in the way of your agenda?

3. Who do you blame when you don't get your work done?

4. Can you tell the difference when you've chosen the good portion?

CHAPTER 3

Who
Do We Work For?

The Bible alone declares that human beings by their very nature are worshipers and that everything that we say and do is shaped by worship.

Paul David Tripp[1]

All of this effort...for who? Who do we work for?

WHEN WE WORK FOR OURSELVES AND/OR OTHERS

> Beware of practicing your righteousness before other people in order to be seen by them, for then you will have no reward from your Father who is in heaven. (Matt. 6:1)

Feeling distraught recently, I dramatically fell on the couch at the end of the day and said to my husband, "You didn't even see all the work I did today." My husband said to me, "Well, sweetheart, God sees you."

Um, yeah, thanks husband. His faith-filled and gentle reminder was a gift, encouraging me that I do not work alone. God is with me. God sees. My little tantrum exposed my heart.

---

1   Tripp, Paul. *Instruments in the Redeemer's Hands* (Phillipsburg, NJ: P&R Publishing, 2002), p. 70.

I often work with one boss in mind—me. My little (or big) daily plans are seen by and executed by *me*. Independent and driven, I set out to do *my* day. No wonder I feel empty and dissatisfied at the end of it. No wonder I look for someone to praise my work; I am searching for meaning, rewards, appreciation. I am a horrible boss.

Working for appreciation or acknowledgement leaves us empty—we are working for a cold taskmaster that will not give us a reward. Rarely do we work well and receive encouragement from our boss. For the stay-at-home mom, it is almost never.

Sometimes, our need for praise and appreciation from people steals our heart's focus and makes us easily forget that God does see us and is always supplying our needs. It is His presence that is ultimately satisfying, yet we forget. Even the most sincere acknowledgment from those near us gives no life. Even if my husband noticed and complimented my efforts every day, my heart would not ultimately be satisfied. Our hearts long for a deeper connection and satisfaction for our work. We need to know who we serve and who we work for. We serve Jesus; we work for Him.

WE NEED TO KNOW WHO WE WORK FOR

> Whatever you do, work heartily, as for the Lord and not for men, knowing that from the Lord you will receive the inheritance as your reward. You are serving the Lord Christ. (Col. 3:23-24)

The Holy Spirit is with us as we do our mundane tasks, unseen by others. God is worshiped as we work heartily for Him. He sees us, guides us, loves us.

I look out at the audience from the stage of my life and I see many people whose approval motivates my work to be well done. Fear of man is a sin that I am very familiar with, but by God's grace, I am being changed into a woman who fears the Lord more (what *He* thinks of me matters most).

> Fear of man lays a snare, but whoever trusts in the LORD is safe. (Prov. 29:25)

WORK MOTIVATED BY FEAR OF MAN

If I have a heart motivator of fear of man in my work, this is what my heart looks like: driven to please others

- concerned with outward appearances more than love and inward affections

- performing to impress: my kids, my husband, my friends, family, etc.

- controlling my environment to attain false satisfaction

- controlling people to attain a false contentment

- using things and people to make myself feel good about myself

- caring too much about the opinion of others or my opinion of myself

- unrealistic standards for home, productivity, relationships that are law-driven not Grace-driven, legalism!

- producing results for praise from man

These heart motivators produce:

- unrighteous anger for any block from standards or productivity to happen

- disappointment when praise from man doesn't happen

- bad feelings about self when tasks don't happen

- inflexibility, irritability

- shame if identity rests on performance

In contrast, through repentance, fear of God in my work looks like:

- desiring first to please God in work

- aware of God in the details

- depending on God in the details

- gentleness and self control

- quiet whispers of prayers when interupted

- tender-hearted conversations that come at the suprise moments

- giving God the credit in my heart for a completed task or simply Him enabling me to do anything

- showing people near me my need for Christ to do anything

- confessing sin quickly

These heart motivations (because of grace) produce:

- Meekness

- Humility

- Self-control

- Kindness

- Love

- Worship

We are working for God. He is more than a good boss. He is a perfect and intimate master. He has called us to work not for ourselves or others, but for Him. Sometimes, we resist this truth. We work hard and sometimes hardly work. When we work apart from worship, we are hiding from God.

WORKING HARD OR HARDLY WORKING: WE HIDE FROM GOD

It is easier for me to work aggressively through a task list than it is to stop and pay attention to those in my presence. Eager hands and cold heart. Cold to the people in my home, ignoring chances to connect, I work faster; feverishly doing, not tenderly connecting. Like Martha (Luke 10), I fixate on my work, causing ambition to cloud my heart from worship. It's interesting to me that I would rather break a sweat with physical labor than peacefully replace my tasks with pursuit of the people I love.

I know work has to be done sometimes, yet I choose to work too much. Let's explore the "too much."

Driven to accomplish, we work without worship when we are cold to the Holy Spirit, ignoring the prompting to love Jesus and others through our work. Who has ever worked dutifully without acknowledging whom we are serving? Busily preparing, cleaning, processing, whatever it is, we are prone to disconnect our hearts from our tasks. In a sense, we are hiding in our work. Instead of our need for God being exposed, we cover ourselves in the busyness of agendas. We can easily hide from God, ignoring Him and those around us.

At the other extreme, we hide from God when He has asked us to work and we choose to be idle. We approach our days lazily, forgetting that God is watching, with us, and loving us. Called to care for people and things, we apathetically hide instead of worshiping. Work nags us, and we ignore the One who called us to work.

In both cases, our action or inaction stems from a belief that God is not with us and hasn't called us to worship Him in our work. Every thought, feeling, belief, action, and motive is seen by God. He gives us His Spirit to guide, comfort, and convict us throughout our days. Instead of recognizing this grace and seeing Jesus, even in the mundane tasks, we go through the motions of schedules, projects, and relationships. Whether we are driven or lazy, we miss Jesus in either case when He gets sidelined.

Why We Work

The good news is that, for the believer, Jesus gives us His perfect job review. His flawless work takes the test for us and in His divine majesty, He clothes us with His righteousness, which is a precious inheritance (Col. 3). We don't get the inheritance because we worked hard—we will always fall short. God's free and perfect saving grace is given to anyone who believes, no matter what the resumé says. On the cross, Jesus took our work ethic, our fear of man, our shame, our pride, and paid with His life.

Jesus has given us His Holy Spirit, who enables our lives to give glory to God. It is the Holy Spirit who fills my heart with wonder and reverence from the mundane to the exciting parts of my day. The Holy Spirit convicts me of sin and turns me in the other direction. Work can only be worship when enabled by the Holy Spirit.

No audience, no approval, no relationship, and no productive day can compare to the gift, the *inheritance*, of God's grace in Christ Jesus. *He* is my reward. Every dish, diaper, errand, relationship, act of service, sacrificial commitment, every job undone or well done, can be offered as an act of worship. Depending on God to accomplish His glory in us and through us is a glorious opportunity that we get! Work is worship not because it is done well. It is worship when my heart is tuned to the presence of a holy and loving God who is glorified by my dependence on Him in all that my hands are called to do. As I worship, my work is transformed from tasks to glory.

WOULD YOU WORK DIFFERENTLY IF YOU REALLY BELIEVED GOD WERE WITH YOU?

Life swirls around us and we sometimes muster up the courage to grab some time to stop and rest. Schedules, tasks, duties, relationships, budgets, errands, ministry, friends, birthdays all capture our attention. A whirlwind of time and memories flashes behind us.

If all of these moments were a race, what would be at the end? What are we racing toward or for? There are many piles of work, and the piles never go away. We run faster and harder in this race of days to get through it all, yet what is getting my body in action? The sweat drips down and the busyness increases—for what?

What is at the finish line? What is all this effort really about? Why do we strain to get through it all? No one seems to notice my straining, since everyone else running beside me is dripping with motivated strides.

Then, I stop and look around to get perspective. I see myself burdened with a heavy load, perspiring, and about to cry from exhaustion. I see others doing the same. Some are sitting down, faces streaked with tears of despair. There are some who are veering off the track to another destination; a distraction of some sort. Others look peaceful, as if they were already done; just resting and glad about it. I look ahead and I see no finish line, even though I was promised it was right ahead of where I stopped! A race that never ends? What did I sign up for? This race is exhausting.

Thus is the race of our Christian faith; specifically, my roles as wife and mother. What waits for me as my reward? What motivates my heart to work hard? Throughout the day, what drives me? What is my rest and peace? What are my eyes focused on?

> Your work is a very sacred matter. God delights in it, and through it he wants to bestow his blessings on you. This praise of work should be inscribed on all tools, on the forehead and faces that sweat from toiling.—Martin Luther[2]

JESUS IS OUR REWARD
How does the good news of the gospel change the way that we work?

1. We are humbled by our weakness and look to Jesus who is strong.

2. We can repent of independence and self-sufficiency and instead cling to God because of the reality that we can't do anything without Him.

3. We work knowing that God sees us and loves us as we serve Him through serving others.

---

2   As quoted in Ewald M. Plass, *What Luther Says* Vol. 3 (St. Louis: Concordia, 1959), p. 1493.

God is the reward. He is the motivation. There *is* a finish line, and our home in heaven is waiting for us. And along the way, as this race exposes our weakness, we can worship Him.

God wants me to run this race of life with endurance. He has set before me this body, this life, this heart to look to Jesus. I run hard for nothing if I am not looking to Jesus. Jesus is the why of my worship: the object, the reward.

> Therefore, since we are surrounded by so great a cloud of witnesses, let us also lay aside every weight, and sin which clings so closely, and let us run with endurance the race that is set before us, looking to Jesus, the founder and perfecter of our faith, who for the joy that was set before him endured the cross, despising the shame, and is seated at the right hand of the throne of God. (Heb. 12:1-3)

I work myself up to a pretty great rhythm and my breathing seems right for the pace, then all of a sudden, I get anxious about the hills ahead of me. My breathing becomes more labored and my heart starts to get discouraged. I whisper, "I can't go any further."

So it is with work. Just as I get my house organized and the laundry caught up, I am staring at overwhelming and steep hills of work ahead of me. What keeps me moving forward growing in endurance? It can only be Jesus that moves me.

God is with me now, not just at the finish line. He is with me with every move I make, every thought, every tender feeling. He is the Promised Land, but I am already there. In Christ, I am both running *toward* Him and *with* Him.

REFLECTION QUESTIONS

1. When the Spirit of God reminds you of Jesus while you are scurrying around trying to accomplish work, what would it look like for you to lean into Christ in the middle of your busyness?

2. Think of a time when you have been exhausted and overwhelmed by your work. How would knowing that God is with you and is your reward for your work encourage your heart to persevere differently?

3. What rewards are you seeking in your work, other than Christ?

4. How might you be reminded of the gospel in your work?

CHAPTER 4

Ambition:
Selfish or Godly?

Work requires action and action requires motivation. In this chapter, we are going to explore attention, action, and ambition—how each of these things can be worshipful.

WHAT OR WHO DO WE GIVE OUR ATTENTION TO?

Right now, (hopefully) your attention is on reading this book. Your mind is engaged and you are here, with these words.

When you are working, you are giving your attention to your work. Most people's minds have to be attentive to the task they are doing or the relationship they are experiencing in the moment. Some of us can do many things at once, but most of the time our attention is clearly on our action in the moment.

For me, my attention is grabbed by (in no particular order):

- Tasks (home, projects, cooking, cleaning, shopping, errands)

- People/Relationships (God, husband, kids, friends)

- Me (working out, beauty, food, reading, prayer, writing)

- Ministry (counseling, meetings, teaching)

- Homeschool (planning, teaching, cleaning, organizing, researching)

- Fun (date night, playing games with kids, watching television, social networking)

Of those things, does any one get more attention than is fitting?

I give a lot of attention to my home, husband, children and my friends. Details concerning my home and family flood my thought life. Needs, prayers, and actions circle my mind and invite me to take action. At some point, those thoughts turn to desires. And when I desire to achieve, I become *ambitious.*

My desire to accomplish makes me ambitious. And whatever I am ambitious for is what I give my attention to. If I am ambitious for a clean kitchen, my thoughts and my hands will be motivated for a clean kitchen. Eventually, my kitchen will be clean. Ambition fuels my action until the work is done. If I am ambitious for a loving relationship with my husband, my heart will be motivated to give attention to that relationship. My ambition—prompts attention—which prompts action.

DOES YOUR ATTENTION FIT WITH GOD'S LOVE AND PLAN FOR YOU ON A DAILY BASIS?

Somehow, my attention often gets distracted and near-sighted. Like Martha in Luke 10, I can lose sight of the big picture so that my eyes only see what is right in front of me. Even worse, I grumble about whatever is in front of me. I forget what to be ambitious *for.* God often shows me my misplaced or neglected ambition by convicting me of my aimless or arrogant ambition.

Occasionally, I get really ambitious for order. My attention is glued on cleaning, organizing, and keeping things running smoothly. On the one hand, this is stewardship that is worshipful. On the other hand, it sometimes is a signal to me that my heart has become more concerned with order than worship—revealing my selfish ambition.

My attention is a signal about what I worship, like a flashing warning sign, and my heart's distraction is glaring. What I give my attention to is what I think is important.

Attention and ambition are close companions. What I give my attention to is likely where my ambition is.

If I am ambitious to redecorate my living room, my thoughts, actions, and motivations will be to accomplish the living room redo. It will get my attention because I am ambitious for it.

Ambition can be worshipful (we will talk about the difference between selfish ambition and godly ambition). And sometimes, our attention proves aimless or arrogant, which is selfish ambition.

SELFISH AMBITION: AIMLESS OR ARROGANT?

Are you aimless with your thoughts? Mental loops, random tasks, or the typical busy brain waves tend to cloud our vision. Distracted from the present, we daydream in a world where the floors are clean, those books get read, and we are ten pounds lighter. Jolted back to reality, we fix our attention on our work. Busily working, but still discontent with the "now," we feel ambitious. But something is wrong. We wouldn't likely admit it, but we are ambitious for our own needs and desires. We love to see a clean house or deadline completed.

When we complete our tasks on time and in a way that meets our own expectations, arrogance can sneak in. As the boxes are checked, pride can carry us to the next action item. The ambitious heart seeks the next challenge, and self-sufficiency is commonly the energy that drives our achievements. Self-confidence and self-sufficiency often motivate us, instead of worship and dependence on God.

Some of us know we have much to do and are super busy. Busy, but not actually accomplishing much. Attentive, yet aimless with our attention. Ambitious, but not dedicated. We work, work, work, yet our work is not focused and prioritized. Like running on a treadmill, we are exhausted but aren't going anywhere. Others of us are ambitious for much and are working hard, but are not acknowledging where our help comes from (Ps. 121).

Selfish ambition is striving to accomplish anything for our own end, our own glory. It is a cold and empty lie that cheats us out of worship. We want to make *ourselves* look good, not Jesus.

God has a lot to say about selfish ambition. Let's take a look.

The former proclaim Christ out of *selfish ambition*, not sincerely but thinking to afflict me in my imprisonment. (Phil. 1:17)

Do nothing from *selfish ambition* or conceit, but in humility count others more significant than yourselves. (Phil. 2:3)

But if you have bitter jealousy and *selfish ambition* in your hearts, do not boast and be false to the truth. (James 3:14)

For where jealousy and *selfish ambition* exist, there will be disorder and every vile practice. (James 3:16)

I sin in selfish ambition often. I am usually blind to it. I get driven and go so fast that I don't even stop to check in with God. Persuaded by check boxes instead of God, my ambitious heart beats to my own drum—self-glory, not God's. In my selfish ambition, my aim is to feel the effects of success, not worship.

Most of us *want* to live out of a godly vision for the details of our lives, but we find ourselves off course – straying from that passion for Jesus and conviction in our hearts. Our attention swerves off the road, and we forget where we were headed. We lose perspective, and our attention grows lazy and unintentional. We work, do, and check things off the list, yet our hearts lose focus and are turned away from Christ.

AMBITIOUS FOR GOD'S GLORY

As Christians, we have a deep down (sometimes ignored or suppressed) appetite for God's glory. Each of us has different expressions of worshipful response. When we plan our lives and actions, we must pray for wisdom and ask: *Am I worshiping Jesus with this? Is my hope to make Jesus look impressive?*

If we love God's glory, our lives will display a lifelong, passionate quest – in other words, godly ambition. Growing in worship means that we are growing in giving God glory in our everyday lives. The grace of God wires us for godly ambition because our worship has action.

Ambition inspired by the Holy Spirit invites us to "do" for *His glory*.

Merely sprinkling Bible verses and prayers on my ambitious striving and calling it "godly" doesn't make it godly. So, what does godly ambition look like? How is ambition worshipful?

1. God created us to be ambitious, for *His* glory.

2. He wants us to work hard, steward well, and exercise wisdom with dreams, plans, and actions.

3. Ultimately, all that we *do* or *dream* is for Jesus to look good, not us.

4. God knows me personally, and the gospel transforms my heart, plans, and dreams every day.

5. The grace of God is where I get my approval; my justification before God is my peace.

6. Striving toward worship in my actions, prayers, and dependence on Jesus refines and defines my motivation to accomplish.

Sometimes, we are all too aware of our temptation to selfish ambition, which can make us fearful to act. We can be aware and humbled by our sinful tendencies with ambition and still take action.

> True humility doesn't kill our dreams; it provides a guardrail for them, ensuring that they remain on God's road and move in the direction of his glory.—Dave Harvey[1]

As we move closer to Jesus, He faithfully guides our motives to act and glory is given to Him.

---

1   Harvey, Dave, *Rescuing Ambition* (Wheaton, IL: Crossway, 2010), p. 14.

Are You Worshiping Jesus with Your Ambition?

My relationship with work is complicated. I don't just work and worship. I tend to grab the glory for myself when I accomplish work, and I tend to work by willpower and self-sufficiency rather than humble dependence on God. Just yesterday, I felt proud with all that I had done in one day. Pride sucks out the humility, and my arrogance kills worship. God is working on my heart, showing me my selfish ambition, and re-routing my sinful desires to godly ambition (= worship).

> Such is the confidence that we have through Christ toward God. Not that we are sufficient in ourselves to claim anything as coming from us, but our sufficiency is from God, who has made us competent to be ministers of a new covenant, not of the letter but of the Spirit. For the letter kills, but the Spirit gives life. (2 Cor. 3:4-5)

We can worship with our ambitions as we strive to see God glorified through us. In humility, we can offer our accomplishments as acts of worship, grateful for His grace at work in us.

REFLECTION QUESTIONS

1. Who or what gets your attention?

2. In your day, what do you think about the most? What are your top priorities? Tasks, relationships, conflicts, worry? How about dreams or fears?

3. When you set out to do a task, are you mindful of God, asking for His aid?

CHAPTER 5

From Overwhelmed
to Overjoyed

OUR LIVES ARE OVERWHELMING

Most women are overwhelmed with what God has put in their lives to care for. We race around with a long list of errands, people to think about and pray for, numerous pressures, "shoulds," and a constant reminder that there is never enough time in the day to do all that we would like to do. Overwhelmed, for most, is an understatement. We feel in-over-our-heads, inadequate, unable, and simply under-qualified for our own lives.

If you are feeling overwhelmed like me, dig in and depend on Jesus. He not only understands our situation, He gives us grace to depend on Him:

> Since then we have a great high priest who has passed through the heavens, Jesus, the Son of God, let us hold fast our confession. For we do not have a high priest who is unable to sympathize with our weaknesses, but one who in every respect has been tempted as we are, yet without sin. Let us then with confidence draw near to the throne of grace, that we may receive mercy and find grace to help in time of need. (Heb. 4:14-16)

REDISCOVERING WEAKNESS

I am not talking about the pitiful, pushover, lazy, weakling kind of weak. I am talking about the kind of weakness that we all inevitably meet when we reach the end of our energy, time, or emotional and/or physical strength. This kind of human weakness is good for us to recognize in ourselves, as long as it turns our hearts toward Jesus.

Weakness in Scripture has sub-categories like: insults, hardships, troubles. We have all experienced trouble. When we do, we don't feel strong, do we? That weakness we experience is a heart acknowledgement that we are not powerful or strong—we need a strong Savior to carry us through. Weakness, biblically, is an honest assessment of how we experience ourselves.

> But he said to me, "My grace is sufficient for you, for my power is made perfect in weakness." Therefore I will boast all the more gladly of my weaknesses, so that the power of Christ may rest upon me. (2 Cor. 12:9)

Instead of hating weakness, we are invited to embrace it as an act of worshipful dependence on Jesus. We need Him to be strong for us!

> For the sake of Christ, then, I am content with weaknesses, insults, hardships, persecutions, and calamities. For when I am weak, then I am strong. (2 Cor. 12:10)

I DESPISE WEAKNESS

Relational debt, housework debt, and the dread of some procrastinated project sneak up, drain the life out of me, and leave me feeling discouraged and flat-out weak. Those overwhelming moments reveal my true weakness. Yet too often I deny it. Blind with my ambition, I reach for my bootstraps, pull myself up, and get back to work.

My heart naturally resists depending on God when I am weak. The noise in my heart, amplified by tough self-sufficiency, can drown out the Holy Spirit's reminder: "My power is made perfect in your weakness."

Yet Weakness Is a Gift

And then there are the times when the Holy Spirit's voice breaks through the noise and exposes my heart. It is a struggle to swallow my pride and obey, but in that turn of repentance—right in the midst of the mess—I begin to hope again.

The truth is, I am weak every second, not just when I feel overwhelmed. Jesus wants me to see that when I am overwhelmed, He is giving me a gracious gift: awareness of my constant need for Him. Rather than despising weakness, I can boast in it, because it draws me closer to Jesus in worship.

God meets me at the point of my prideful self-sufficiency and lovingly brings me to my knees in worshipful dependence.

The other day, I was scurrying around the house getting stuff done, feeling very behind on my seemingly urgent tasks. Our third child invited me to play dolls.

Pause.

Graciously say "no" or accept this opportunity to connect with my daughter? In the moment, overwhelmed with my work, my heart was faint. I thought, "I can't play right now!" Yet, the Holy Spirit changed my thoughts to dependence and flexibility in my weakness.

Feeling overwhelmed is a signal to check my heart's dependence on God. Am I softened to the Holy Spirit? Am I digging in to depend on God? Do I find my soul's refreshment in God's sufficiency? In these times, I'm learning to cling to my Savior who accomplished perfect work on the cross and continues to save me from my sin. God meets me at the point of my prideful self-sufficiency and lovingly brings me to my knees in worshipful dependence.

My daughter and I had a great time playing. When I went back to work, my heart was more tender than before.

We Must Boast in Our Weakness

Worship through work is not *just* working hard for God's glory; it is also an attitude of humility, realizing how weak and unable we are. We can all grow in dependence on Christ and boast in our weakness by humbling ourselves before the face of God and thanking Him for that gift. His power is made perfect in and through our weakness, as we claim the strength of Christ.

Practically, as a mother—this battle rages each day. Instead of embracing my weakness and worshiping Jesus in it, I choose other options. Even if you are not a mom, you might relate to the following experience responses when overwhelmed.

MANAGER, MARTYR, OR MEEK?

When pressed, strained, and overwhelmed, I become: a *manager*, a *martyr*, or a *meek* mother.

Manager Mom

Cold and process-oriented, this mom sees her kids like a task list. Bathed? Check. Fed? Check. Sibling conflict resolved? Check. Happy? Check. This is the kind of mom-heart I have when I am overwhelmed and feeling out-of-control. It is difficult for me even to look up from my work and smile at my kids when I am Manager Mom.

Once, when I was harried and focused on "my agenda," my husband asked me a question, and I blurted, "I'll get to that babe, but first I need to *process* the children." Blurts often reveal my sinful heart. More than people to "process," my children are image bearers of God: people I am called to represent Jesus to by loving, serving, protecting, and guiding them. Seeing our kids as check boxes is one way my heart responds to feeling overwhelmed. I can tell that I am Manager Mom when I am not relationally connecting with my kids and when my goal for the day is to be super-productive rather than to enjoy them.

My desire to control the environment often misses my children's hearts as I focus on completing tasks instead of looking in their eyes, playing a game, or being silly. Duty-driven, my heart is more concerned with clean floors than a heart that fears God, which would incline my heart to my children's hearts.

I embrace the lie that I can help myself.
Manager Mom's goal? To accomplish.

Martyr Mom

Pitiful and grumbling, this mom sees her kids as inconveniences. Feeling isolated and despairing over the insurmountable amount of work that fills her days, she compares all aspects of her life to others' seemingly easy lives. This is the kind of mom-heart I have when I feel lonely.

While it is a blessing to stay at home with my children, it can be lonesome. Even on loud days when the children are constantly talking, arguing, crying, or making some kind of noise, my soul can still feel sad and lonely. Facing various challenges with homeschooling or cleaning projects, emotional burdens, and too much to do, I feel inadequate and weak. I look around for someone to blame. Is it the mess-makers (my kids), or is it my husband? Offended at the amount of work before me, I grumble.

Martyr Mom leaks anger and ingratitude. I know I am slipping into Martyr Mom when I am apathetic about Jesus. My time with God is dry or non-existent. I'd rather _____ than find my worth in Christ alone.

I embrace the lie that no one will help me.
Martyr Mom's goal? To sulk.

Meek Mom

Feeling weak and overwhelmed, this humbled mother sees her children as gifts that cause her to depend on Christ. Reminded by inadequacy, Meek Mom tenderly turns to Jesus as her strength. This is the kind of mom-heart I have when I am conscious of God, repentant of sin, and asking for help.

My best days as a mom are when God humbles me amidst the nagging noise of my work. I get overwhelmed easily with how much God has called me to steward. It is too much for me to do—and that is the point. I can't maintain my home or family apart from Jesus giving me grace to do so. Meekness is magnified in my heart when I submit that truth back to Jesus. I cry out to Him for help and He helps! The Holy Spirit comforts and calms, changes my posture, and reminds me of my hope. Meek Mom fears the Lord and is aware of His steadfast love, nearness, and help.

I embrace the truth that God is my helper.
Meek Mom's goal? To depend on Jesus.

FROM OVERWHELMED TO OVERJOYED
So, what about joy?

What does it look like to move from overwhelmed to overjoyed? Or you might ask, "How can I, a stressed-out worker, have joy?" If I were sitting across the table from you, I would look in your eyes and gently remind you that reaching the end of your perceived strength is a gift from God. When you are aware of your weakness, you can truly worship. Embrace that weakness!

Jesus wants us to place our overwhelmed hearts before Him, and He truly does give us strength. His power is made perfect in our weakness. Off our high horse, humbled, and aware of need, we call out to God to be our strength for us. Great is His faithful care for us, and He not only gives us strength, but also joy. We move from overwhelmed to overjoyed when we see Christ as our daily strength. We depend on Him, love Him, and want to be with Him.

REFLECTION QUESTIONS

1. When burdened and overwhelmed with responsibilities, what kind of person are you?

2. How does weakness tempt you in your relationships?

3. When does joy characterize your heart?

4. How might you embrace your weakness and God's strength?

CHAPTER 6

Less Control,
More Worship

Made in the image of God, we are invited to worship in all aspects of our lives, understanding He is sovereign and knows what is best for us. Realizing His control is good is one thing; repeatedly giving Him the "reins" of our lives is another. We can trust God to love us in our mess.

"Neat" Never Happens

Believing we are in Christ—women of God, created in Christ Jesus for good works—we strive to live lives to love and glorify our God. If Jesus is our treasure, do our lives continually reflect this rich grace? Often, we experience joy and peace as we go about our complex lives, trusting Christ with the details. Other times, we take the reins and figure that, actually, *we* would be better managers of the chaos. So, we try to create order in the mess, happy little compartments that we suppose will bring peace.

But, it isn't that easy, is it?

Our lives aren't neatly arranged. We try for "neat" and it never happens. Rather, our lives are messy, filled with stacks and piles, chaos, and busyness. Our hearts are full of wandering desires distracting us from Christ, making those good works and loving acts of service sometimes non-existent or simply scattered across the disorder of our lives. And, our life stories are broken and complex, never easily understood. So, we limp through life as Christian women, searching for "balance" amidst the chaos.

Often, our response to the mess is to create compartments in our hearts. We make the lists: house, marriage, kids, extended family, schedules, friends, food, hobbies . . . and Jesus (Interesting how Jesus gets his own separate compartment!).

Mental compartments give us a sense of order for our overwhelming lives. Our minds continually race through the various categories, checking items off our lists or not, gladly tucking devotional and Bible-thoughts into that "Jesus" category. Feeling weak and inadequate with what we haven't gotten done, we wrestle with who we are in the disorderliness. As we struggle with hope and feel condemned by what is lacking, Jesus seems distant, unavailable, and cold. We briefly acknowledge Him and then get back to work, sure that God will understand our mess.

No Time for Jesus?

We may have heard that "all of life is worship." Clueless for how to achieve this, we try to "do more" worshipful thinking and feeling, hoping maybe if we do more in the Jesus-category, it will somehow overflow into the others.

That can't be right, can it? Do we think if we ever "get it all done," we will have time left over for God?

Our attempt to gain order by compartmentalizing or controlling our lives, people, and tasks is really a heart issue. We have to ask ourselves what we believe. Do we believe that God is Lord over all, attentive to us in everything? Does He care about the details, the insignificant aspects of our lives? Does Jesus really care about our lawns or laundry?

What gets you up in the morning? Do you awaken to the sound of your alarm, or the gentle tapping of a toddler on your arm? As you get out of bed, beginning your day, what do you look forward to? What motivates any of us to rise from our slumber?

What Is Your Agenda?

There are many mornings I would love to put earplugs in and just sleep! For those of us with young children at home, a full night of satisfying, restful sleep is a rare commodity. Waking up in the middle of the night to feed a baby is part of the job, and it is worship. Worship, because God loves your baby, and when you love your baby, you are doing what God wants! Waking up to read, exercise, or get a jump start on your work day can all be worship. Whatever season you are in, God has called you to worship in it.

For me, I have four children and a husband. God has put before me a home to manage and a family to care for. I can't just "willpower" myself out of bed! That will only last so long before I grow bitter and resentful at what God has called me to. The motivation has to be more than just waking up to do whatever the day requires of me. There is a deeper and more meaningful purpose in our work. There is always a list to accomplish or a schedule for the day. Yet, the list isn't enough. Willpower is shallow. It only leads us to the next goal. We get stuck and never quite reach the destination. Left frustrated, we keep striving.

THE CONTROLLER

Our sister, Martha, in Luke 10, was a controller. She lost sight of her aim to worship Jesus, and instead, her goal became the task, her work, the preparation of the meal. Jesus loved her and spoke truth to her (I can only imagine how Jesus' rebuke humbled her) until the day she died. I wish I could spend the day with Martha and ask her questions about her heart that day. I can relate to the tattle-taling heart that resents when others experience a freedom to engage and flex on tasks. The temptation to control my environment comes daily.

The Controller can eventually relax only by submission (yes, submission) to Christ. God can turn our selfish ambition to ambition for worship. I am starting to see how precious His grace actually is and how near my Heavenly Father is to me. I can calm down, enjoy the freedom to be flexible, and worship Jesus in and through my work more quickly.

I can trust Jesus to lord over my life, arrange it all. He has it all under control. Martha had God in the flesh pointing out her sin of controlling and her misplaced worship. Jesus was gracious to her, and the same Lord is being gracious to me. In His grace, I find my hope that He can change my heart. I stand in joy and belief that as my heart is broken over sin, Jesus' death and resurrection—I can trust Jesus to sanctify me.

I probably will always (given my personality) tend toward selfish ambition and the desire to control my environment. But Jesus is changing me. He is redeeming my desires, turning my control into worship.

WORSHIP IS MORE THAN A SONG

How do we make the shift from Controller to Worshiper? Actively handing the reins over to our attentive God (He already has them, anyway) is the first step. We can tenderly acknowledge our propensity to compartmentalize and can pray for discernment, that we may see our distracted worship and desperate need for Christ. We need the Holy Spirit to help us to see how we have pushed God aside in our effort to "do" our own lives (John 14:26).

Worship is more than a song or posture. "Christian worship is the response of God's redeemed people to his self-revelation that exalts God's glory in Christ in our minds, affections, and wills, in the power of the Holy Spirit."[1] Worship is that turn of focus from my agenda to His and seeing Christ made great in my thoughts, actions, and feelings—to gaze on Him through the details of life.

WE SERVE—WHATEVER, WHENEVER, HOWEVER

To worship Jesus throughout our stressful, busy days without putting Him in some compartment means we truly see Him as Lord over all of life, deeply loving us in the details. Yes, even the mundane tasks of our lives! Remember Colossians 3:23-24:

---

1   Kauflin, Bob. "Defining Worship, Pt. 2," *Worship Matters*, November 7, 2005, http://www.worshipmatters.com/2005/11/07/defining-worship-part-2/, retrieved December 10, 2012.

"Whatever you do, work heartily, as for the Lord and not for men, knowing that from the Lord you will receive the inheritance as your reward. You are serving the Lord Christ."

So, whatever, whenever, however we serve, we are serving King Jesus.

> Worship is the believer's response of all that they are—mind, emotions, will, body—to what God is and says and does.— Warren Wiersbe[2]

If we love Jesus, we can relinquish control, knowing that our holy, perfect, and attentive God is Lord over all these self-made compartments and gives us His Spirit to demonstrate His wisdom and grace daily. We are invited to live this out, as worship.

Pause for a moment the next time you are doing dishes, reading a board book to your toddler for the thirtieth time, filling your car up with gas, attending another boring meeting, cleaning toilets, pulling weeds, or lying down for sleep, and think of our God who is with you. He loves you. His control is trustworthy and safe.

REFLECTION QUESTIONS

1. Have you put Jesus into a separate category or compartment in your life? How would it change your day-to-day living if you considered that He is really part of all of your life? What would that look like practically?

2. Have you ever been in the middle of controlling something and then realized you were horribly incapable of succeeding without Christ? If you relented, and gave whatever it was over to Jesus, what was that like? With that feeling in mind, can you envision giving over everything to Him, even the things you *do* feel like you can manage?

---

2   Wiersbe, Warren. *Real Worship* (Grand Rapids, MI: Baker Books, 2000), p. 26.

3. Take a moment and pray for the Holy Spirit to give you discernment over the areas of your life where you tend to keep things for yourself rather than turning them over to God. Talk with someone else about what is revealed to you and ask them to help hold you accountable as you seek repentance in an area that is sinful and to remind you of God's grace.

Chapter 7

"Heart" Battles:
Fighting to Worship

You Are in a Battle Right Now

You might be feeling a little stirred up, uncomfortable, or simply annoyed. If you've been reading along wondering where I am going with all of this talk of work and worship, let me pause for a moment and remind you.

The point of this book and my heart's desire is not to simply give you the "how-to's" of work and worship. But it is my prayer that my words would be accompanied by a work of the Holy Spirit that brings you to a deeper place of conviction.

When we hear truth, we either gratefully embrace it or push away, bristling. We read Scripture with warm expectation, wanting truth to fill us. We love God, His word, relationship with Him, and the truth that gives us life. Sometimes, though, we hear truth and it shines a mirror in an area that makes us cringe. We don't want to see what God has in mind for our lives or, more importantly, our hearts. Yet, if we love Jesus, we are willing to look in the mirror again and see the Holy Spirit filling us with hope that yes, even though we are uncomfortable, we can embrace the truth and the uncomfortable change that truth requires.

The battle comes when God lovingly shows us our struggle, yet we reject the confrontation and deny the sin. Like a toddler whose toy has been snatched away, we panic when our idols are exposed, fearful about how we will survive without them.

When we are uncomfortable, we need to be reminded that Jesus is exposing our sinful hearts as a gift so that we can be restored and clean. It is often the Spirit showing us sin in our lives. He also shows us our distorted view of God. The truth of the gospel gives us life, because if we remain in our sin, the result is death. We need to be saved from our sin and ourselves. We all need Jesus to renew our hearts first; then, our behavior will follow. Lasting change follows heart change.

WE ARE DESPERATE FOR CHANGE

Broken people (which all of us are) want change. Devastated by sins done against us and despairing in sinful responses, we desire to be redeemed from it all. We want freedom from pain, suffering, and condemnation. For Christians, change is linked to repentance. Our brokenness translates into godly sorrow, which brings heart change. We desire to be different. We want to be like Jesus. We don't want to sin. In most cases, change happens slowly. Gradually, our thoughts, motives, desires, and behaviors are altered by the Holy Spirit as we trust God to change us.

When a believer is stuck in a rut, there's a frustration with self. We take a look at ourselves and fixate on the problem. A solution is in order. We anxiously survey the "self-help" options like an overweight person perusing the diet ads. Motivated by wanting a fix for our broken self, we shop around. Redemption, then, becomes a desirable product to be purchased. As though watching an infomercial, we are inspired by the before and after's, hoping for and coveting results. Except, it isn't weight loss we're after; it's our hearts that need change.

YOU CAN'T BUY REDEMPTION

Redemption is about the Redeemer, but so easily we make it about the results. We often want His gifts more than we want Jesus Himself. Redemption isn't a commodity; it is what God does for us that results in our transformation. One can want redemption, but redemption begins and ends with Jesus. It is a subtle yet significant difference to see people thirsty for redemption's results *rather than* craving the Redeemer for lasting satisfaction. We are tempted to focus on being changed rather than fixing our heart's gaze on Christ.

For example, the self-aware sister that finds herself frustrated in a perplexing cycle of condemnation and temptation wants out. She wants change. She might be enticed to be more curious about self-analysis than repentance and relationship with Christ.

The people-pleaser gal that finds she never measures up to the expectations of everyone in her life might be tempted to dutifully work out her change-process instead of focusing on Jesus, who is already pleased.

Wanting redemption more than wanting God is a delusion. Because God loves us beyond our comprehension, we can't fathom the scope of redemption that is available in Christ. Like missing the forest for the trees, our vision is blurred when we fixate on change and miss Jesus. We can't bring redemption to ourselves or muster up change. We need a miracle.

IT'S ALL GRACE

Tempted to "fix ourselves" (which is impossible), we focus on the "change-process" instead of the "changer" Himself. His grace makes redemption possible.

> In him we have redemption through his blood, the forgiveness
> of our trespasses, according to the riches of God's grace, which
> he lavished upon us. (Eph. 1:7-8)

God promises He is faithful to redeem us by lavishing grace upon us. Through the blood of Jesus, we are changed, we are loved. Believing that God's grace is abounding, we need to remind others to not be dazzled by the change-process, but to fix our eyes on Jesus wholeheartedly. Jesus already bought redemption for us, and we can stand in confidence. He has lavished His love upon us. We can gaze at His face, changed by His grace, and believe that He will (eventually) change us into His image.

JESUS BOUGHT MIRACULOUS REDEMPTION

You are already loved. Redemption is as certain as Christ's glorious resurrection! As heart change happens, so can our realization of the miracle that occurs. Jesus died in our place for our redemption. His blood was shed so that ours wouldn't have to be. He endured the cross so that we wouldn't have to pay the penalty for sin. Often, we stumble through life ignoring this miracle of redemption. Instead, we work for it on our own. Before we know it, we've put God on the sidelines in the game we play of becoming a "better person." Change is inevitable as the Holy Spirit is given room to transform us. Repenting to Jesus ignites the grace that God freely gives us. Our hearts are changed because God intends for us to become more like Jesus. Jesus is our only true redemption.

WE CAN'T CHANGE OURSELVES

For the sluggard that longs to have an organized home and not feel buried every day, there is hope. You feel overwhelmed and ill-equipped to get your life in order; Jesus promises to help you. Ask Him—He is ready and willing to guide your heart and give you wisdom, relationship, and faith to try new things. Fear will decrease, and your humbled heart will shine as His strength makes you strong. Neither your weakness nor your inadequacy define you; they give you a shortcut to see Christ's strength made perfect through you (2 Cor. 12:9-10).

For the busy and fun girl that never says "no" to people, but desperately wants the freedom that comes from choosing the good portion, you can believe that Jesus will give you courage to say no and trust Him to define who you are, not who people want you to be. Time is running out: run to Jesus and find your true rest.

For the happy church lady that always makes a "joyful noise" but doesn't do the mundane tasks with the same joy, you can repent of spiritual pride for *appearing* worshipful but not humbling yourself to approach the insignificant parts of your life with a cheerful heart, even when you are unseen by others. You may try to impress others with your "churchyness," but your religious ways don't point us to Jesus. God is gentle and kind. Grace invites you to relax and know that He loves you when you aren't even trying.

For the "leave-me-alone-get-'er-done" girl, you don't have to be so strong. Although your intention may be to keep burdens from others, your independence may actually cause greater difficulties, and it may push other people and God out of your life. We all need both other people and Jesus. The gospel is for people that actually need saving. That is you too! Jesus will gently remind you that grace defines you, not your work. Your vulnerability is a gift to those that love you. I hope that you know how loved you are. Jesus rescues you.

For the bitter, wounded sister, you've been sinned against and you haven't come to Jesus with your pain. You love Jesus, but dark grudges bury your heart and your work is apathetic and cold. Sometimes, you work hard, but your effort is for yourself to look good, for others to be pleased. Worship will be when you believe you are accepted because of Jesus' perfect work, alone. He took your shame and loves you intensely.

For the dear friend that doesn't know Jesus, I love how driven you are, yet you worship yourself. You were made in the image of the Creator and you represent His grace beautifully, yet your aggressive self-worship is a dead end. All this selfish ambition and morality is meaningless. Only Christ satisfies our endless desires. All other gods will fail you. I pray you meet Jesus, the only true lover of your soul.

These are all women I know and love. They battle and struggle in their hearts to worship Jesus. I have cried with countless women, seeing their toils, the misplaced hope, all reminding me that our common heart struggles lead to the same place: our desperate need for Jesus to be our identity, our hope to cling to.

TRUE LASTING CHANGE

As we are changed by Jesus, there is often evidence of His grace at work in our heart. While there will always be struggle, we can be thankful that we are not defined by our Struggle but by our Savior. Here are some examples of evidences of being changed:

- Desiring God

- Wanting to see Jesus Christ from the mundane to the significant parts of our lives

- Repenting quickly as the Holy Spirit gives us awareness and conviction of sin

- Depending on God, and those He has placed around us, to provide insight, encouragement, and help as we mature

- And, my favorite theme in Scripture: fear of the Lord!

That is where we are headed next, and I am really excited about what's around the next bend!

REFLECTION QUESTIONS

1. When was the last time you "cringed" when you heard a truth about an area of your life and/or heart that the Holy Spirit was convicting you to change? What was your response and what did you do?

2. How can you look to Jesus, the Redeemer, rather than the result of the redemptive work?

3. Share with a friend, family member, or neighbor a time that God brought true, lasting heart-change to your life. How does your heart feel when you share how abundant God's grace is with someone else?

PART TWO:

A Woman
Who Fears the Lord

CHAPTER 8

Imitate, Don't Idolize

Worship is a biblically faithful understanding of God combined with a biblically faithful response to him. Conversely, idolatry is an unbiblical, unfaithful understanding of God, and/or an unbiblical, unfaithful response to him.

Pastor Mark Driscoll[1]

When we hear the word *idolatry*, we often picture tribal people erecting poles or lighting candles in some statue-god's honor. Far from primitive times and artificial worship, idols of the heart can be anything in our lives that replaces the one true God.

WHAT IS IDOLATRY?

When we replace Jesus with anything else in our hearts—our affections, time, thoughts, decisions—we reflect what we worship. As we survey our lives, we often find God-replacements. Stop right now and ask yourself, "What do I want today? What is frustrating me about myself today?" I'd bet that many of you have

---

1   Driscoll, Mark. "What is Idolatry," The Resurgence, http://theresurgence.com/2011/01/11/what-is-idolatry, retrieved December 10, 2012.

a swirl of self-judging and comparing thoughts. For example: "I never get as much done as her."

But as Mark Driscoll states, quoting Tozer, "Idolatry is simply worship directed in any direction but God's, which is the epitome of blasphemy."[2] When we make people into an idol in our hearts, we put their opinions, love, and acceptance above God's. We may not physically be bowing down to them, but we crave time with these people and demand their attention. The desire of our control-hungry heart is to possess our idol; thus, instead of loving them, we actually crave possession of them as an object. This could be someone close to us like a spouse or a parent. Or it could be a leader, a friend, or someone we don't know—perhaps someone famous. At some point, admiration for the person merges with desire to be like the person, and we make the person an idol as we worship him or her.

As a young woman, I was a fragile new believer and longed for examples of godly families or women to learn from. The desire to learn from women was good. God blesses us with Christian families so that we can be encouraged by their examples. However, my desire to be like one specific older woman stopped feeling encouraging and instead became a sinful pressure I put on myself to be like her. *Imitation became idolatry.*

Imitation keeps Jesus as the goal. Idolatry makes being *like that person* the goal. For me, being like this friend became more motivating than being like Jesus. I'm not immune from this temptation even now. From Martha Stewart to the Proverbs 31 woman, my heart is easily persuaded to idolize. Idolatry of a particular woman usually brings self-condemnation, because I feel inferior to my superior assessment of the woman I am worshiping. Instead of feeling encouraged, I feel that I will never measure up. For some, it is a made-up image of the woman we long to be, and our imagined perfection is the goal. Or it's ourselves in perfected form.

We see this sometimes with women's events and groups. These events often communicate the formulas for "How to Be

---

2   Tozer, A.W. *Purpose of Man* (Ventura, CA: Regal Books, 2009), p. 55.

a Christian Woman," and often the subtle unspoken pressure is to be the five things that "she" embodies. On the stage in our heart is the "Christian Barbie®" with her perfect worship, home, family, and heart. We leave feeling isolated and inadequate unless we were encouraged to live lives centered on the gospel and grace.

Is it wrong to give godly examples of how women worship Jesus? No, but we must be reminded in our hearts of the warning not to idolize, and instead to imitate godly women as they point us to Jesus.

Who have you made into an idol? Who has motivated the way you live your life as a woman?

What Is Imitation?

More than just copying, Scripture tells us there are good examples of people who fear God and walk in faith and wisdom. We are told to be encouraged by their lives and to fight for a faith in Jesus like theirs. Imitation feels like a fresh breeze of grace, as we are encouraged to live to glorify God. This helps us see what worship looks like. The New Testament says:

> And we desire each one of you to show the same earnestness to have the full assurance of hope until the end, so that you may not be sluggish, but imitators of those who through faith and patience inherit the promises. (Heb. 6:11-12)

> Beloved, do not imitate evil but imitate good. Whoever does good is from God; whoever does evil has not seen God. (3 John 11)

So, who do you imitate? Does she encourage you to worship Jesus through her example? Paul and John in these Scriptures (enabled by the Holy Spirit) urge us to imitate godly people, for the fruit of a godly person's life is worth imitating. Imitating someone is seeing her life lived in humility and worship; we can learn from, be sharpened by, and enjoy the example that the godly set by pointing us to Jesus. The purpose of imitating anyone is to draw us closer to Jesus. Paul expressed this truth as follows:

Brothers, join in imitating me, and keep your eyes on those who walk according to the example you have in us. (Phil. 3:17)

We Are Called To Be Imitators of God

Therefore, be imitators of God, as beloved children. (Eph. 5:1)

As we watch others that point us to Jesus, we imitate the fruit of the Spirit in their lives as part of our worship of Him. We are called to be imitators of God because we are His children. As God continues to love His kids, we get to shine His love to others.

In the next chapter, we are going to spend time understanding the Proverbs 31 woman, but we must remember we are invited to imitate, not idolize, her characteristics.

REFLECTION QUESTIONS

1. Is there a woman you look up to and admire as an example? What about her do you most want to imitate? Do those qualities point you to Jesus? What about her do you tend to idolize? Are those God-glorifying or world-embracing qualities?

2. What godly characteristics do you see in yourself?

3. How can you grow in imitating Jesus? Try to think of one or two ways.

CHAPTER 9

Jesus is Greater than
the Proverbs 31 Woman

Ok, sisters. I dare you to read Proverbs 31:10-31 twice. The passage is included below. Pay attention to your heart's reaction. Notice when you feel inspired or intimidated, or when your mind tunes out the words because it just seems like too much to absorb, or when you feel like you are already so familiar with this passage, you don't expect to learn anything new.

Ok...go!

Proverbs 31:10-31:

[10]An excellent wife who can find?
She is far more precious than jewels.
[11]The heart of her husband trusts in her,
and he will have no lack of gain.
[12]She does him good, and not harm,
all the days of her life.
[13]She seeks wool and flax,
and works with willing hands.
[14]She is like the ships of the merchant;
she brings her food from afar.
[15]She rises while it is yet night
and provides food for her household
and portions for her maidens.
[16]She considers a field and buys it;
with the fruit of her hands she plants a vineyard.

[17]She dresses herself with strength
and makes her arms strong.
[18]She perceives that her merchandise is profitable.
Her lamp does not go out at night.
[19]She puts her hands to the distaff,
and her hands hold the spindle.
[20]She opens her hand to the poor
and reaches out her hands to the needy.
[21]She is not afraid of snow for her household,
for all her household are clothed in scarlet.
[22]She makes bed coverings for herself;
her clothing is fine linen and purple.
[23]Her husband is known in the gates
when he sits among the elders of the land.
[24]She makes linen garments and sells them;
she delivers sashes to the merchant.
[25]Strength and dignity are her clothing,
and she laughs at the time to come.
[26]She opens her mouth with wisdom,
and the teaching of kindness is on her tongue.
[27]She looks well to the ways of her household
and does not eat the bread of idleness.
[28]Her children rise up and call her blessed;
her husband also, and he praises her:
[29]"Many women have done excellently,
but you surpass them all."
[30]Charm is deceitful, and beauty is vain,
but a woman who fears the LORD is to be praised.
[31]Give her of the fruit of her hands,
and let her works praise her in the gates.

Now how do you feel? Excited? Charged with mission? My guess is that you aren't exactly invigorated. Why is it that this section of Scripture doesn't entice us to jump up and down with enthusiasm? Perhaps you might be feeling a little torn right now. Half intrigued and half cynical. You are not alone. This experience is a common and real tendency in the hearts of the women I know, and certainly in myself.

If the Proverbs 31 woman sounds like a biography of you, I have two questions for you:

1. Are you humble in your abilities, giving God the credit each step of the way?

2. Are you serving Christ by serving other women, encouraging them towards worship?

My prayer is that your strength, capabilities, and gifts would be exhibited through meekness.

For every other woman, the background message of this passage is the "shoulds" of the Christian women's culture. When we participate in this culture, we say to ourselves, "I *should* be like the 'Proverbs 31 woman.' She is amazing, what is my problem? Why can't I get up before my family and prepare for the day? Where is my 'field to consider and buy'? I *should* serve with a godly heart like that. I *should* serve the poor. Do I open my mouth with wisdom?" These "shoulds" replace the Lord's intention for us to see godly behavior that is worthy of imitation, and to be encouraged and inspired. Instead, we feel inadequate and ashamed.

First things first.

As we consider this passage in more detail, join me by praying that your mind would be silent from these "shoulds," distractions, and lies as we consider why the Proverbs 31 woman makes us squirm. I am sensitive to the way women (including me) add to the Scriptures and respond with the familiar condemning "shoulds." Remember, God chose to include this in the Bible. But His way with us is not to load "shoulds" on our shoulders; He is gracious and loving.

Pray for a tender heart, ready to accept encouragement. After we deal with the intimidation factor, let's work together on being humbled and inspired as we encounter these words from the Lord.

PROVERBS 31 WOMAN: WE ARE INTIMDATED, NOT INSPIRED

The Proverbs 31 woman wasn't one woman. She was written as Wisdom personified. Wrongly, tragically, and sometimes blindly, we make being like her (not Jesus) our goal. This superwoman is untouchable, intimidating, and too good to be true. We think, *if we want wisdom, all we have to do is study her and hope that somehow we become awesomely wise.* Who wouldn't want to drip wisdom and gentleness, all the while managing her home and family with calm and grace?

> She opens her mouth with wisdom, and the teaching of kindness is on her tongue. She looks well to the ways of her household and does not eat the bread of idleness. (Prov. 31:26-27)

We look at her and are mesmerized and a little perturbed. We compare ourselves to this idealized woman and feel inadequate, envious, and overwhelmed. Of course we desire to be godly, we want to worship Jesus, and we would love to have it "all together"—but surely there is a shorter route to being like her!

This Excellent Woman was written as an acrostic; perhaps to help a ruler remember his alphabet when he was young, and know what admirable qualities he should look for in his future wife.

Our Goal Isn't to *Be Her*, It Is to *Be More Like Him*

As your vision is corrected, look clearly at your goal. It isn't to grow into this perfected woman, or even close. You will never be her. So, shake her off. Be freed up and cling to this truth: Jesus will make you more beautiful, holy, wise, and a precious demonstration of grace the more you love Him. He is the goal.

Aiming for Wisdom, We Often Miss Jesus

What we often want is a shortcut, a formula, a model, a method for achieving results. Whatever the problem, we want the solution to be efficient and effective. We are often persuaded by the "before and afters," enticing aromas, and quick-fix schemes. Beauty and perfection (airbrushed images) lure and lie to our hearts, tempting us to us to attempt being like "her."

When it comes to being a "Christian woman" or the "Proverbs 31 lady," there is often a strong desire to become or look like what we think "she" is. She, then, becomes the image of our comparison. Furthermore, we just replace the glamor girl on the magazine with the Christian girl. If there were a "Christian Barbie®," we would own her. She isn't real, yet we get sucked into the lie and believe it is actually possible to look and be like her.

Instead of being inspired to worship Christ more holistically, we turn that inspiration into idolatry. We use the very thing meant to encourage, turn it on ourselves, and sin.

Jesus Is Our Wisdom

[B]ecause of him you are in Christ Jesus, who became to us wisdom from God, righteousness and sanctification and redemption. (1 Cor. 1:30)

Jesus *is* our wisdom. He perfectly embodies the wisdom of Proverbs 31. And we are being made to be more like Him. One of the great hopes of our sanctification is precisely that as we become more like Jesus, we become more wise, because He *is* wisdom. Which is to say, the more we become like Jesus, the more we become like the Proverbs 31 woman.

And as we worship, when we lay down the false god of being a "Proverbs 31 woman," being like Jesus becomes the goal of our hearts. Life is found in Christ alone, who is our only hope for wisdom. Worshiping Jesus makes us wise, because He is wise.

As we continue to the next chapter, "A Woman Who Fears the Lord," I want to remind us again that these qualities are worthy of imitation, not idolizing. Pray for the Holy Spirit to keep you focused on Jesus as the goal of your worship, not on being a particular godly Woman. Loving Jesus is enough. His grace defines you—*not* being like "her."

REFLECTION QUESTIONS

1. What particular traits or characteristics of the Proverbs 31 woman do you admire most? How can you imitate and not idolize those traits?

2. Which particular traits or characteristics do you think are the least attainable for you? Journal about what is weighing on your heart when you think about them.

CHAPTER 10

Fear of the Lord

*Fearing the Lord means that this worshipful awe is
the single and unchallenged motivator of everything
I think, desire, say, and do.*

Paul Tripp[1]

FIGHTING FEAR

Fear is a complex topic. There are legitimate and illegitimate
fears, sinful fears and a holy fear (fear of the Lord). Knowing
women, and my own heart, I don't think there is a grander, more
pervasive heart-struggle than fear.

In counseling women, I have found that the majority of issues
a woman faces connect to fear. I have heard "I am afraid" so many
times. Fear from troubles and pain from the past, present, or
potential future—we all struggle to have peaceful instead of fearful
hearts. Sometimes, fear can be chaotic and irrational, and other
times, it can be subtle and so familiar that we don't even notice it.

Fear is an all-consuming, truth-altering threat. It robs us of
peace.

---

1   Tripp, Paul David. *A Quest for More* (Greensboro, NC: New Growth Press,
     2007), p. 126.

The only remedy to the fears of this life is fear of the Lord. But, before we get too far down that track, I want to share a personal story:

I have struggled with fear, in various forms, all of my life.

Alone, afraid, and living in a turbulent home at age thirteen, I sought shelter under my blankets. Confused and weighted with burdens beyond my maturity, I tried to be strong, alone. There was no one I could turn to—until Jesus made Himself known to me and gave me new hope. I had recently become a Christian, but had no idea this newfound peace would be tested so soon.

In the midst of facing my familiar daily fears came the shocking news: my grandmother had been murdered. It was terrifying. I was grieving this loss and haunted by the evil that brought it. The darkness of this tragedy shrouded me. Daily life seemed gloomy. How would I survive? How do any of us survive the hardships and threats of life? I needed a shelter from the storm. I longed for help. Fear gripped me.

> God is our refuge and strength, a very present help in trouble. Therefore we will not fear though the earth gives way, though the mountains be moved into the heart of the sea. (Ps. 46:1-2)

As insurmountable trouble in my home and heart attempted to steal my hope in God; it felt as if the earth were giving way. Exhausted and weak, something began to shift in my heart. God was inviting me to find safety in His arms. Scared and tenderly calling out for help, my rescuer was near. I had to fight my fears with fear of the Lord. My fight was gentle and weak.

FIGHTING FOR FEAR OF THE LORD

God ignited a fight in my heart to not give in to fear, but to trust His love to protect me. To be assured that He would fight for me. Beautifully, God confirmed to me that He is all I need. All other potential saviors were stripped away. False hopes, security, love, comfort—all absent. I realized that it was just Jesus and me.

Suddenly, my heart filled with hope. If all I had was Jesus, I had everything. Jesus is my God, and He loves me. He is my rescuer, redeemer, and a very present help in trouble. No amount of chaos can steal my salvation in Christ (Rom. 8:38-39).

That all happened twenty-two years ago, though I remember it like it was yesterday. Joy had replaced the darkness in my heart as I ran to my refuge. Often, I still struggle with fear today. But, with God Himself as my shield, my battle is always won. Fear of the Lord is a beautiful and brutal battle of the heart. As long as I live, sneaky fears of this life will try to threaten the safe place of trusting in God. To fight those fears is to believe Christ has already won the battle and will continue to redeem my heart in the midst of it.

WHAT MAKES YOU TREMBLE?

What brings awe-filled tears to your eyes? What stops you in your tracks, causing you to ponder deeply? When are you likely to nervously yet joyfully obey God? My guess is that in all those answers, your heart beats with the fear of the Lord. Fear of the Lord is being aware of Him, His power, and His constant attentive love for us, His children. It is the deep yet tender acknowledgement of a Holy, Perfect God that causes us to tremble with wonder, reverence, and worship.

> "Fear of the Lord" means reverent submission that leads to obedience, and it is interchangeable with worship, rely on, trust, and hope in. Like terror, it includes a knowledge of our sinfulness and God's moral purity, and it includes a clear-eyed knowledge of God's justice and anger against sin. But this worship-fear also knows God's great forgiveness, mercy, and love. It knows that because of God's eternal plan, Jesus humbled himself by dying on a cross to redeem his enemies from slavery and death. It knows that, in our relationship with God, he always says, "I love you" first. This knowledge draws us closer to God rather than causing us to flee. It causes us to submit gladly to his lordship and delight in obedience. This

kind of robust fear is the pinnacle of our response to God.—
Edward Welch[2]

Fear is a powerful experience, potentially robbing us of peace and trust in God's care for us. Fear of the Lord is, instead, our heart's anchor to the goodness of God.

> The fear of the Lord is the beginning of wisdom. (Prov. 9:10)

It is a sweet, satisfied emotion that rests in the awe and presence of God. Knowing His wrath, His judgment, His power, His holiness, His grace, His sacrifice, His faithfulness, His tender mercies, His riches, we worship and bow in reverence, in fear. Fearing God is that deep, slow, cleansing breath that we take when we believe: *God has me safe in His arms. He is working this circumstance out, because He loves me.* If the fear of the Lord were our heartbeat, then other fears wouldn't grip us like they tend to.

However, other fears do often rule us. Real threats in life attempt to steal our hope in God and our security in His love. Embracing other fears is forgetting the fear of the Lord. Forgetting our true refuge in God, we flounder in the face of our situation. We forget Almighty God is reigning, ruling, and keeping us close.

What fears are in your life? How can you replace them with fear of the Lord? What everyday threats in your life are causing you to doubt whether or not you are protected in your Father's care?

We experience fears of all types. One of the things that I have feared is wind: wind that is so powerful, it gusts 50 miles per hour and causes the giant evergreen trees towering and surrounding our house to sway, dropping branches on and around our home…it terrifies me! Some people have said, "Wind storms are cool" or "The loud sound of the wind is peaceful." What??? Some winters, I have allowed the fear of the wind and the trees to be so controlling in my heart, I don't trust God to protect me,

---

2   Welch, Edward T. *When People Are Big and God Is Small* (Phillipsburg, NJ: P&R Publishing, 1997), p. 97.

my family, or our home. Fear can be irrational. Fear can be all-consuming. Fear can seemingly take over our thoughts.

Every winter we experience wind storms, sometimes so powerful that they bring a giant evergreen tree or two down. On days that it isn't windy, my heart can experience more peace. I know that fearing God means that, even on the wind storm days, my heart can be in the same place as on the "still" days. To fear God is to trust Him and His power over my fear of the wind: to experience calm and rest because God is keeping me safe.

The last couple of windy seasons, my wind fear has decreased as fear of the Lord has increased! I have bathed in psalms that talk about God being our fortress, refuge, safety, rock, and stronghold. As God has supplied my heart with His fatherly care, concern, lordship, and strength, I am starting to get it. There is no formula for replacing one fear for the right fear. Yet, in God's grace, He has calmed my fears as I have placed more trust in God's power, protection, specific love for me, His wrath, His kindness, and His mercy. This transition isn't easy. I have to fight for this trust and fear. I have to tune my heart to the music of Psalms 27, 31, 61, 71 and believe the words!

REDEEMED FEAR

In the same way that paying attention to the wind stirs my fear, which motivates me to hide from the wind, fear of the Lord motivates me to hide not *from* Him, but *in* Him. Fear of the Lord is worship, because His holiness is traumatic, bringing me to my knees in awe, wonder, and submission. When I realize my Father is watching and keeping me safe, I can run to Him in any trouble.

> The fear of the LORD leads to life, and whoever has it rests satisfied; he will not be visited by harm. (Prov. 19:23)

> For the LORD your God is God of gods and Lord of lords, the great, the mighty, and the awesome God, who is not partial and takes no bribe. (Deut. 10:17)

When any of us are afraid, we need to fight for fear of the Lord. It is a temptation for me, for all of us, to not fight and instead, to linger in doubts, insecurities, and the unknowns. But, we are charged to fight in response to fear (1 Tim. 6:12). It is a battle to take off the blinders of the world, to fight against indwelling sin, and to resist evil (Eph. 6:12).

Recently, a surprise early fall wind storm hit us. There was a power outage, and a giant tree had split in half and was resting on trees near our vehicles. The wind was so loud, you could hear the branches splitting. Jesus worked on me. I felt peace. Instead of getting anxious, I went to Psalm 121, read it out loud to my kids, and prayed silently that I would trust God and have peace in my heart. I took a nap!

Now, that my friends, is redemption! It snuck up on me. Later, I shared with my husband how I didn't worry, and then realized that I was growing in the fear of the Lord.

Like a fountain of life (Prov. 14:27), the fear of the Lord gives us grace to believe that we are loved. Without the fear of the Lord, our hearts lack the deep root of faith, which secures our peace.

REFLECTION QUESTIONS

1. What fears in your heart push aside fear of God?

2. Are you afraid of fear of the Lord? Does it seem like giving something up?

3. God is lovingly inviting you to see a glimpse of His holy love for you, what would it cost you to embrace Him?

CHAPTER 11

Works with Willing Hands

She seeks wool and flax,
and works with willing hands.
She is like the ships of the merchant;
she brings her food from afar.
She rises while it is yet night
and provides food for her household
and portions for her maidens...
She looks well to the ways of her household
and does not eat the bread of idleness.

(Prov. 31:13-15, 27)

She seeks, works, brings, rises, provides, looks well.

As we continue to look at the characteristics of the Proverbs 31 woman—characteristics worthy of imitation—we are zeroing in on being productive and purposeful in our daily life as part of our worship of Jesus. First, let's look at the heart behind this woman's behavior in light of what Jesus says about service.

Jesus said in Mark 9:35, "If anyone would be first, he must be last of all and servant of all." His mission was to lay down *His* life for *His* sheep (John 10:11-15). He came not to be served, but to serve (Mark 10:45).

Her Servant Heart

Willing

> She works with willing hands…(v. 13b)

She works willingly, not begrudgingly. If we are honest, we know that the moment we wake up, we are needed. Our schedule starts the moment we wake up. Whether it is our work place or our homes and families, we are presented with constant opportunities to serve. If you have small children, you may be up off-and-on all night. Grumbling and procrastination could easily characterize our days. But, instead of putting off work, we are invited to work hard, willingly, heartily, as worship. Are you *willing* to work? Are you accepting God's invitation to serve Him by serving others?

Humble

> Humble yourselves, therefore, under the mighty hand of God so that at the proper time he may exalt you. (1 Pet. 5:6)

When we are humble, we have an honest assessment of ourselves. We know that we are loved, and we respond to that love by loving God and others right back. When we believe God and accept His grace, we are humbled. Humbled, because of our weakness and need for Him. Humbled, because of His greatness and our dust-ness. "For he knows our frame; he remembers that we are dust" (Ps. 103:14).

We live in the reality of being fully loved and in full weakness: in need of God's strength.

Joyful

> Serve the Lord with fear, and rejoice with trembling. (Ps. 2:11)

When we work joyfully, we have happy hearts. Not just because we have modern appliances and vehicles helping us in our work (though these are wonderful blessings for sure), but because we remember how great our sin is and how great God's love is. We are humbled by our sin and joyful because of Jesus' payment for it. Being forgiven and knowing Jesus stir joy in us. How can we frown when we are loved by God? Our work is an extension of this knowledge. Sure, there are real struggles. But, are we clinging to Jesus who is our joy in the midst of them?

Generous

> She looks well to the ways of her household...(v. 27)

She gives generously and sacrificially as she serves God by serving her household. She doesn't just do the bare minimum; she goes beyond the expectation. She looks for ways to make her household feel cared for, personally. She is generous with her time and attention to detail.

> Give generously to them and do so without a grudging heart; then because of this the LORD your God will bless you in all your work and in everything you put your hand to. (Deut. 15:10, NIV)

Confident

Again, the fear of the Lord is her foundation. She stands so firmly in who God is, that doubt is far from her heart. She can serve Him and her household with an unwavering confidence. She isn't a confident woman because of her abilities, but because God has loved her.

> In the fear of the LORD one has strong confidence, and his children will have refuge. (Prov. 14:26)

This lady, worthy of imitation, loves God. Her behavior isn't perfect, but it does flow from a heart that fears the Lord. Her confident, generous, joyful, humble, and willing heart produces fruitful behavior as worship unto God. These behaviors aren't just "willpower," but worship. As her heart fears the Lord, her work is worshipful.

Her Servant Behavior

She Provides

> And provides food for her household and portions for her maidens... (v. 15b)

She has thought through what her household needs for each day, month, and season. She works hard to provide food, clothing, and supplies for her family. Her family trusts her to have thought about what is needed. They don't worry, because she has provided for them.

She Gets Up Early

> She rises while it is yet night. (v. 15)

She gets up before the sun. She has already opened her eyes and heart to God to serve those He has called her to serve. She may still be yawning, but she is up.

But...why?

It is quiet. It is the perfect time to focus, pray, and prepare your heart to serve.

Theologian John Piper says it this way:

> I earnestly recommend that it be in the early morning, unless there are some extenuating circumstances. Entering the day without a serious meeting with God, over his Word and in prayer, is like entering the battle without tending to your weapons. The human heart does not replenish itself with sleep. The body does, but not the heart. We replenish our hearts not with sleep, but with the Word of God and prayer.[1]

She gets up early to get a jumpstart on her work, but more likely the richer pay-off is getting her heart focused in humble service to God.

---

1   Piper, John. *When I Don't Desire God* (Wheaton, IL: Crossway Books, 2004), p. 116.

She Puts Others' Needs First

She is responding to her household and family's needs, all day long. A humble servant, working diligently, joyfully responding to requests. She feels glad to serve others and put them first.

> Do nothing from selfish ambition or conceit, but in humility count others more significant than yourselves. Let each of you look not only to his own interests, but also to the interests of others. (Phil. 2:3-4)

She Is Thoughtful

Her heart is engaged, knowing the people she serves well. Her service to her family is personal. She knows what kinds of food they like, she knows what "extras" make her family feel loved. She is providing the basics, but she is also paying attention to the details of serving her family. She works thoughtfully, because she loves her household.

She Breaks a Sweat

She works so hard, she isn't afraid to break a sweat. She isn't trying to be so prim and proper and have perfect hair and make-up; she can get dirty from work. She pulls weeds and dumps garbage. Vigilantly working, she is not just cleaning, she is worshiping—humbly.

> Whatever your hand finds to do, do it with your might, for there is no work or thought or knowledge or wisdom in Sheol, to which you are going. (Eccles. 9:10)

Motivated By Grace

Are you feeling exhausted by this list of characteristics? If so, I want to remind you of God's grace. His grace guides us through these characteristics of a woman who fears the Lord, inviting us to imitate—as an act of worship. It is so easy to look at this list and feel inferior. We need to remember that it is Jesus whom we worship. The Proverbs 31 woman reflects Him. As we worship Him, we grow to reflect Him too. We *imitate* her, motivated by

His grace; but we *worship* Him, not her. We are staring at Jesus, not this list.

There is a sweet freedom in inspiration that is built on grace instead of the law. If we see ourselves loved by Jesus, not for anything we have done but solely because of His grace, then our worship flows freely and gratefully. But, if the law (doing to get love) motivates us, we may feel inferior, condemned, and self-righteous when we accomplish something.

WHAT SHE ISN'T

Working to Get Approval or Love
She isn't serving her family so they will love her. If they forget to say "thank you" when she does something for them, she isn't crushed. Her hope is not in how her family views her. She can serve them joyfully, as an overflow of her joy in God. Her self-image is not in her work, home, or how her household sees her. But, her self-image is her affection for God. Simply, He loves her, so she loves Him back by serving. Work is a response to God's love. Work is worshipful as she focuses her heart on Him.

Mustering Up Willpower
She doesn't have a motivating mantra for her hard work, claiming super-strength to accomplish her days. Even if she did for a time, the willpower would eventually die. White-knuckling never works. Willpower isn't *real* power. We will talk later about how godly discipline is different from willpower. For now, know that this exemplary sister isn't vowing to work hard in her own power, but is drawing on the Holy Spirit for strength.

WHAT SHE IS INVITED TO: A HEART THAT WORSHIPS
Jesus is our perfect example of both a servant's heart and servant's behavior. His demonstration of humility and sacrifice invites us to worship. As we look to Him, the author and perfecter of our faith, we can respond with worship. Working hard, humbled, and joyful—we steward what He has entrusted to us.

REFLECTION QUESTIONS

1. When are you most likely to "white knuckle" your service to others?

2. When do you typically take your quiet time to be with God? What would it look like to wake even ten minutes earlier to have prayerful reflection with Him in preparation for the day?

3. How could cheerful, willing service to others impact your relationship with them?

CHAPTER 12

Meekness:
True Strength

*Trying to do the Lord's work in your own strength
is the most confusing, exhausting, and tedious of all
work. But when you are filled with the Holy Spirit,
then the ministry of Jesus just flows out of you.*

Corrie Ten Boom

Everyone wants to feel strong, right? Culturally, we embrace
strength as a virtue, celebrating our might, power, and victories.
Individually, we like to think of ourselves as invincible, never
taking "no" for an answer. We pretend we aren't getting old
and refuse assistance from others, all in the name of perceived
strength from within.

While it isn't a sin to want to be strong, we need to recognize
our actual state of being: deep-down weakness. I hope that you
can join me in not only embracing the truth of our individual
weakness, but learning to worship Jesus in it.

Always Weak

Pushing ourselves and those around us to meet deadlines,
routines, tasks, lists, and goals, we often do everything we can
to get to the "productivity finish line." *Too slow?* YOU LOSE!

Only the fast, ambitious people win, right? The longer you take to think about what you are doing, the further behind you are. Our task list whips us as we trudge forward in wet cement.

Sometimes, the pressure tempts us to escape, give up, or become bitter. Discouragement and despair set in and we quit trying. It is just too much. Something deep within cries out in need. We would rather lose than push ourselves to accomplish what seems impossible. Tired of the stress, the burden, and the strain, we slowly lose focus. Becoming apathetic seems like the best route. We definitely see our weakness, our need. Unsure of what to do with ourselves when we are weak, we numbly move on.

Or, self-sufficient action kicks in. Our weakness is exposed, but we decide we don't like feeling needy. Coldly, we push God to the side, embrace independence, and vow to get things done out of sheer will. A fierce work ethic fuels our fire to accomplish our day's tasks. Confronted with challenges, we are tempted to clutch an "I can do it!" mentality, trusting ourselves, not Christ.

Either way, God is not in the picture. Both heart responses reveal independence from God. When our weakness is realized, it is a gift of God's grace. The truth is, we *were* weak even before we *felt* weak.

> But he said to me, "My grace is sufficient for you, for my power is made perfect in weakness." Therefore I will boast all the more gladly of my weaknesses, so that the power of Christ may rest upon me. For the sake of Christ, then, I am content with weaknesses, insults, hardships, persecutions, and calamities. For when I am weak, then I am strong. (2 Cor. 12:9-10)

Once we realize that we are weak, the best possible response is to accept this reality and to turn to God for strength.

WEAKNESS CAN BECOME MEEKNESS
Sadly, weakness and meekness are two very misunderstood ideas and are often associated with "pansy, needy, fearful, cowardly."

Perhaps like me, you have filed these words under "what I don't want to be like."

Aspiring to either seems strange to me, yet the Bible describes both meekness and weakness as admirable qualities for anyone to embrace. When we realize our weakness, we are acknowledging both our human frailty and need to be saved. We need Jesus.

EMBRACING WEAKNESS

> Blessed are the meek, for they shall inherit the earth. (Matt. 5:5)

Instead of despising our weakness, we are invited to embrace it as an act of worshipful dependence on Jesus. Acknowledging our weakness can be worshipful as we pursue Christ in it, leaning into Him for strength.

God's power is made perfect in our weakness; when we recognize our weakness, our pride melts and our posture becomes meek. This meek demeanor displays Christ's power instead of our own perceived strength. David, Moses, Abraham, Paul, and even the Lord Jesus were described as meek. We are in amazing, holy company when we become meek.

1. Two important truths should fill our minds daily: God is all-powerful, I am not.

2. I cannot do anything without the enabling grace of God.

MEEKNESS = DISPLAYING CHRIST'S STRENGTH

Meekness, like weakness, often comes with negative associations that make us uncomfortable. Yet, if King Jesus was described as meek, then we should consider a more inspiring view of meekness.

> The meek man is not a human mouse afflicted with a sense of his own inferiority. Rather he may be in his moral life as bold as a lion and as strong as Samson; but he has stopped being fooled about himself. He has accepted God's estimate of his own life.

> He knows he is as weak and helpless as God has declared him
> to be, but paradoxically, he knows at the same time that he is in
> the sight of God of more importance than angels. In himself,
> nothing; in God, everything. That is his motto. He knows well
> that the world will never see him as God sees him and he has
> stopped caring. He rests perfectly content. —A.W. Tozer[1]

As we acknowledge our weakness, our posture becomes meek.
Meekness is an outward expression of our deep need for God's
grace, power, and strength. If Weakness says: "I have no lasting
strength or power, but Christ is all-powerful and strong for me,"
then Meekness shows the status and is the proof of that belief.
Meekness, then, is weakness displayed as worship.

This means that meekness is a godly attribute, a description
of a humbled heart. In many places in Scripture, *meekness* and
gentleness are interchangeable or complementary adjectives for
a Christian.

> Put on then, as God's chosen ones, holy and beloved,
> compassionate hearts, kindness, humility, *meekness*, and
> patience. (Col. 3:12, emphasis added)

> I, Paul, myself entreat you, by the *meekness* and *gentleness* of
> Christ—I who am humble when face to face with you, but bold
> toward you when I am away! (2 Cor. 10:1, emphasis added)

> But let it be the hidden man of the heart, in that which is not
> corruptible, even the ornament of a *meek and quiet spirit*, which is
> in the sight of God of great price. (1 Pet. 3:4, KJV, emphasis added)

> But sanctify the Lord God in your hearts: and be ready always
> to give an answer to every man that asketh you a reason of the
> hope that is in you with *meekness* and fear. (1 Pet. 3:15, KJV,
> emphasis added)

There is nothing more beautiful than a meek heart trembling
with fear of the Lord, a heart that knows God is lovingly paying
attention to even the most mundane parts of our lives and hearts.

---

1   Tozer, A.W. *The Pursuit of God* (WLC, 2009), p. 62.

As we bow down before a great God, lay aside our pride and short-lived strength, and accept our weakness, we are becoming meek.

A meek woman is a woman who fears the Lord. Our physical beauty fades, but the glory of Christ in us only gets brighter. Let's aspire together to meekness.

REFLECTION QUESTIONS

1. What comes to your mind when you hear "weakness" or "meekness"?

2. What would you have to give up in order to be meek?

3. Survey your life and heart. Where have you seen meekness?

4. Practically, how would meekness become a personal goal for you?

CHAPTER 13

Mission Minded

She dresses herself with strength
and makes her arms strong.
She perceives that her merchandise is profitable.
Her lamp does not go out at night.
She puts her hand to the distaff,
and her hands hold the spindle.
She opens her hand to the poor
and reaches out her hands to the needy.
She is not afraid of snow for her household,
for all her household are clothed in scarlet.
She makes bed coverings for herself;
her clothing is fine linen and purple.
Her husband is known in the gates
when he sits among the elders of the land.
She makes linen garments and sells them;
she delivers sashes to the merchant.
Strength and dignity are her clothing,
and she laughs at the time to come.
(Prov. 31:17-25, emphasis added)

Dressed with Godly Strength

She dresses herself with strength... The world tells us that power, wealth, health, independence, positive self-esteem, and success equal strength. But the Bible has many different explanations of what strength actually is.

Godly strength is humble dependence on God. God's holiness produces our freedom to be strong because He is strong and He is the one in control. Godly strength involves surrendering our control and trusting His perfect control. Godly strength involves meekness: displaying our weakness and God's strength instead.

A godly woman puts on strength and dignity. This reminds us that, more than our physical clothing, the heart's clothing is the most important and the most impressive. The brightest beauty is from a woman's heart that fears the Lord, shining through even the dullest clothing. Have you ever met a woman who was wearing old clothes and an old-fashioned hair style, yet her heart's light radiated because of her humble posture? Godly clothing is the internal, spotless beauty that streams out of you, showing the glory of Christ.

> Do not let your adorning be external—the braiding of hair and the putting on of gold jewelry, or the clothing you wear—but let your adorning be the hidden person of the heart with the imperishable beauty of a gentle and quiet spirit, which in God's sight is very precious. (1 Pet. 3:3-4)

This beauty is the unseen *fear of the Lord*: strength, dignity, and a gentle spirit. In God's sight, this is true beauty and is of great worth. Our cravings for outward beauty lessen as we desire to walk closely with Jesus. Flowing from that inward beauty, the heart submitted to Jesus will exhibit far more loveliness than a heart gripped by worldly vanity. Inward beauty transcends the fleeting and superficial.

> Put on then, as God's chosen ones, holy and beloved, compassionate hearts, kindness, humility, meekness, and patience. (Col. 3:12)

COMPASSIONATE AND MISSIONAL

She opens her hand to the poor. She is "on mission." And by that, I mean she is aware of the power of the gospel to change lives in her community. She knows that even the smallest actions can demonstrate the grace and mercy of God. With careful attention to her household, her heart overflows out of her house as she responds to the needs in her community. She reaches out to the marginalized. Why is she paying attention to poor strangers? She serves them because she sees people rightly—as image bearers of God.

When you are out in your community, what is your heart's response when you observe the poor? Compassionate? Desensitized? Numb? Prompted by love, we can truly help others know God—by serving and responding to needs. Are you regularly learning what needs there are?

When we respond "on mission" in our community, we are also modeling to our children compassion, service, and ultimately the power of the gospel to change lives. We are showing them how being loved by Jesus compels and enables us to love others.

Are our eyes open to the oppressed, needy, the fatherless? Are we listening for the voice of the Lord, inviting us to adopt His children who need loving families? Has compassion translated into action?

MISSIONAL MIXED MOTIVES

Disordered Priorities

Sometimes, we try so hard to be mission-minded, we neglect our primary mission: our own family. We fulfill requests for help by compromising our time with our families. We might deliver amazing meals for others while feeding our husband and kids cold cereal for dinner. We may spend all day with a woman who needs encouragement, when our children are aching for encouragement from their own mom. If we are "on mission" and are sharing the gospel with our neighbors, we need to honestly consider if we are giving the gospel to our family members first.

Being on mission is always sacrificial; something has to flex so that we can give our time or treasure to others. Therefore, our heart's priorities need careful prayer and discernment as we pursue living "on mission."

Fear of Man

Fear of man—instead of fear of the Lord—can motivate me to serve others: to impress them with great food, compassion, or just consistent love. People-pleasing isn't loving others: it is loving ourselves. If what I get out of giving is gratitude from others, it can easily be a cyclical motivation. Wanting praise and appreciation from others can tempt me to keep giving, because I like how I feel about me when I hear their praise. Giving or serving others, then, becomes selfish, not worshipful.

> In all things I have shown you that by working hard in this way we must help the weak and remember the words of the Lord Jesus, how he himself said, "It is more blessed to give than to receive." (Acts 20:35)

Religious Actions

Sometimes, our acts of service are humble, quiet, and honoring to God. For me, there is often a temptation to proclaim my good deed, wanting to be seen or appreciated. Trumpeting my kindness screams religious pride and overlooks the mercy of God. I steal glory when I announce the mercy *I* have given, when, in fact, it is *God's* mercy flowing *through* me.

> Beware of practicing your righteousness before other people in order to be seen by them, for then you will have no reward from your Father who is in Heaven. Thus, when you give to the needy, sound no trumpet before you, as the hypocrites do in the synagogues and in the streets, that they may be praised by others. Truly, I say to you, they have received their reward. But, when you give to the needy, do not let your left hand know what your right hand is doing, so that your giving may be in secret. And your Father who sees in secret will reward you. (Matt. 6:1-4)

Worshipful, Merciful, Missional Hearts

> Those who doubt God's love for them will not mobilize for mission. Unless we know the Father delights in us even as he delights in Jesus, we will lack the emotional capacity necessary to resist complacency and actively engage in missional living. The only people who can truly turn their eyes outward in mission are those who knowingly live within and enjoy the loving gaze of their heavenly Father. —Dan Cruver[1]

Being on mission to share Christ's love is an honor and gift. It is truly more blessed to give than to receive, and doing so brings sweet worship. Fear of the Lord motivates me to be prayerful and ready when there is a need. My aim isn't to get others' approval or to look righteous, but rather, to have a humble, worshipful heart—because God's grace makes it so. Remember, being on mission isn't *my* mission: it is being on *God's* mission. Our aim is to make *His* name great, and while we act—we are growing in worship.

REFLECTION QUESTIONS

1. When is outward beauty more important to you than inward beauty?

2. Do you dress your heart with the strength of the fear of the Lord?

3. When have you mixed your missional priorities?

4. Do you long to tell someone about something good you've done for another? What can you do instead of seeking praise from others?

5. How could you promote more awareness in your heart and family life of your community's needs?

---

1   Dan Cruver, *Reclaiming Adoption* (Cruciform Press, 2001), p. 18.

6.	Have you ever created a family mission statement? This is a great idea for establishing long-lasting purpose in your family's love for others.

7.	How might you cultivate cheerfulness in serving your community with your family?

Chapter 14

Wise, Worshipful Words

*She opens her mouth with wisdom, and the teaching
of kindness is on her tongue.*

(Prov. 31:26)

We can worship God with our words. We read here in Proverbs 31 of
these characteristics worthy of imitation, flowing from a heart that
fears the Lord. This woman speaks wisdom and teaches kindness.

Before we can speak wisdom *or* teach kindness, we must
know wisdom and kindness. We can't give what we don't know.
You can't teach something that you, yourself, have not learned.
For example, you would never teach a pottery class without
having first held and formed clay into something beautiful. You
simply cannot extend wisdom and kindness if you haven't been
the recipient of it. Before we give it, we must receive it.

Where Does Wisdom Come From?

Look underneath wisdom, and you will find the fear of the Lord.

> The fear of the LORD is the beginning of wisdom, and the
> knowledge of the Holy One is insight. (Prov. 9:10)

Fear of the Lord is the seed that grows wisdom. As we grow in
Christ, our wisdom also grows. Our words begin to resemble

His loving kindness to us. Fearing God compels us to think before we speak, knowing that our words have power to tear down or build up those we desire to love. Words born from the fear of the Lord are most certainly self-controlled, purposeful, and worshipful. We are more inclined to speak wise words when we are submissive to the Holy Spirit.

The Opposite of Wisdom: Foolishness

Proverbs teaches us that if you aren't fearing God, you are a fool. One of my son's bedtime prayers has often included, "Jesus, please give me wisdom." A few times lately, I have noticed him acting with wisdom or saying something wise. I have pointed it out as encouragement, "Buddy, do you see how God is answering your prayers? He is growing you in wisdom!" He just grins and moves on. When we see wisdom coming out of our hearts, we should be encouraged, because we know that the Spirit of God is working in us to grow us into the image of the Son.

Proof of wisdom is truly an evidence of God's grace.

And then there is foolishness. That same son who craves wisdom is still immature (So am I, by the way). He has a snarky habit of saying, "I know, mom." He is deeply convinced he knows so much, and it is as if he physically turns his "listening ears" off and believes wholeheartedly that I have nothing to teach him in that moment. He stubbornly asserts that he already knows what I am trying to teach him.

Last night, this happened again. I sat down on his bed and said, "Remember how God is growing you in wisdom? Well, when you argue and insist that you already know something, when in fact you can still learn more, you are resisting God's wisdom. You don't know everything. There is always something to learn. And if you think you don't have more to learn, you are a fool." His icy posture melted. God's grace was evident in his heart, revealed in his sweet eyes. Nervous, I thought he might cry. I had just called him a fool!

He realized that by ignoring and rejecting insight or knowledge from his mom, he was becoming the very opposite of what he has been praying for. We prayed, thanking God for answering his prayers in a surprising way, showing him the dangerous ditch of the fool—pride.

Seeing the opposite (foolishness) in our hearts is also evidence of God's grace, showing us our need for wisdom. When we see our propensity toward foolishness, we are growing in wisdom. This is what Proverbs teaches in this area:

> ...fools despise wisdom and instruction. (Prov. 1:7b)

> Give instruction to a wise man, and he will be still wiser; teach a righteous man, and he will increase in learning. (Prov. 9:9)

> Whoever trusts in his own mind is a fool... (Prov. 28:26a)

> Do not speak in the hearing of a fool, for he will despise the good sense of your words. (Prov. 23:9)

WISDOM SPEAKS

Wise words reveal a heart that knows the steadfast love of the Lord. God *is* wisdom, and because He loves us, He gives us wisdom.

> Whoever is wise, let him attend to these things; let them consider the steadfast love of the LORD. (Ps. 107:43)

The Powerful Tongue

Our words have the power to express love for God and others or to hurt God and others.

> Death and life are in the power of the tongue, and those who love it will eat its fruits. (Prov. 18:21)

> What man is there who desires life and loves many days, that he may see good? Keep your tongue from evil and your lips from speaking deceit. (Ps. 34:12-13)

> A soft answer turns away wrath, but a harsh word stirs up anger. The tongue of the wise commends knowledge, but the mouths of fools pour out folly. (Prov. 15:1-2)

> And the tongue is a fire, a world of unrighteousness. The tongue
> is set among our members, staining the whole body, setting on
> fire the entire course of life, and set on fire by hell. (James 3:6)

A tongue that speaks wisdom and kindness knows how to both
be on guard and how to be self-controlled. Consistent, godly
speech must come from a changed heart. If our hearts are truly
changed by Jesus, we will hate gossip, slander, and lies. We will
hurt for others when they are wounded by words. Our words
will increasingly represent God, bringing life. On guard and
controlled, we can worship Jesus with our words.

Are You Guarding Your Tongue?
Do you see your tongue as a tool to wield with wisdom? Are
you guarding your mouth from foolish speech? Are you cautious
with the words that you speak? Pray that the Holy Spirit would
help you honor God with your words.

> Whoever keeps his mouth and his tongue keeps himself out of
> trouble. (Prov. 21:23)

> Let the words of my mouth and the meditation of my heart be
> acceptable in your sight, O Lord, my rock and my redeemer.
> (Ps. 19:14)

Are You Controlling Your Tongue?
As you grow in your affection for Christ, he will grow your
desire to please him with a self-controlled tongue. Self-control is
a fruit of the Holy Spirit (Gal. 5:22).

> If anyone thinks he is religious and does not bridle his tongue
> but deceives his heart, this person's religion is worthless.
> (James 1:26).

> Whoever desires to love life and see good days, let him keep his
> tongue from evil and his lips from speaking deceit. (1 Pet. 3:10)

Yet, we need help from the Lord to guard or control our tongue.
We don't have the strength on our own. Eventually, our self-
control wanes and we realize our weakness and inability to

constantly guard our tongue. This is where fear of the Lord meets dependence on the Holy Spirit to keep us faithful to Him. We need the Lord to keep our tongues guarded, controlled, and worshipful.

> Set a guard, O LORD, over my mouth; keep watch over the door of my lips! (Ps. 141:3).

WISE AND WORSHIPFUL WORDS

The goal of speaking wise, worshipful words is to love Jesus and others. As we aim our words, the bulls-eye is loving God.

> [Jesus] said to him: "You shall love the Lord your God with all your heart and with all your soul and with all your mind. This is the great and first commandment. And a second is like it: You shall love your neighbor as yourself. On these two commandments depend all the Law and the Prophets." (Matt. 22:37-40)

Loving God

Here are some ways that Scripture shows us how our words display our love for God.

Boasting of His goodness:

> I have not hidden your deliverance within my heart; I have spoken of your faithfulness and your salvation; I have not concealed your steadfast love and your faithfulness from the great congregation. (Ps. 40:10)

Confession and repentance:

> If we confess our sins, he is faithful and just to forgive us our sins and to cleanse us from all unrighteousness. (1 John 1:9)

Prayer:

> The LORD is far from the wicked, but he hears the prayer of the righteous. (Prov. 15:29)

Loving Others

Here are some ways that Scripture shows us how our words communicate love to others.

Sharing the Truth:

> Until I come, devote yourself to the public reading of Scripture, to exhortation, to teaching. (1 Tim. 4:13)

> Preach the word; be ready in season and out of season; reprove, rebuke, and exhort, with complete patience and teaching. (2 Tim. 4:2)

> Rather, speaking the truth in love, we are to grow up in every way into him who is the head, into Christ. (Eph. 4:15)

Speaking words of healing:

> There is one whose rash words are like sword thrusts, but the tongue of the wise brings healing. (Prov. 12:18)

When we open our mouths, are wisdom and kindness on our tongue? Do you see the opportunity for worship with your words?

I see this more clearly as I shepherd my children. They grumble, shout, demand, discourage, and fight one another. Their sins usually include words. As they grow in wisdom, they are learning the connection to their words. As I help them see their sin, I am often convicted of my own foolish speech. For them to understand the impact of words, both for positive and negative, is a sign of their growth in Jesus.

IF WE KNOW JESUS, THEN WE HAVE WISDOM, BECAUSE JESUS IS OUR WISDOM

> And because of him you are in Christ Jesus, who became to us wisdom from God, righteousness and sanctification and redemption, so that, as it is written, 'Let the one who boasts, boast in the Lord.' (1 Cor. 1:30-31)

Because we are loved by Jesus, He gives us His wisdom. Through the Holy Spirit, we can speak words that love, heal, and help others. We can impact others with words that communicate the love of Jesus.

REFLECTION QUESTIONS

1. Do you see your words as worship?

2. When do you allow your words to be flippant, lacking self-control?

3. Where would God have you submit your words to Him as you grow in wisdom?

4. How does fear of the Lord affect your speech?

PART THREE:

Worship:
Our Response to Jesus

CHAPTER 15

We Need a Gospel Vision

Never be content with your grasp of the gospel. The gospel is life-permeating, world-altering, universe-changing truth. It has more facets than any diamond. Its depths man will never exhaust.

C.J. Mahaney[1]

_____

WE'VE LOST VISION

Why do we do what we do? Most days are filled with work, demands, stress, and arbitrary thoughts filling our mind. Going through the motions of our lives without careful attention to the "why's," we become forgetful. Forgetting the purpose for our actions and relationships, our thoughts become a muddled pool of "someday," "maybe's" and "should've beens." Regret and half-heartedness characterize our self-assessment at the end of our day. We lie awake recounting the actions and the next day's hope for productivity.

As I continue to beat the worship drum, I am inviting you yet again to ask "why?" Are you dissatisfied with the meaninglessness

_____

1 Mahaney, C.J. *The Cross Centered Life* (Sisters, OR: Multnomah Publishers, 2002), p. 67.

of your actions? Christian sister, do you ever confront yourself on how the gospel makes a difference in your daily life? I propose that there is no greater strength or more firm a foundation than the perfect, powerful gospel of Jesus Christ. The gospel is the how, why, and who we live for, infiltrating every aspect of our purpose. Yet, our vision so easily becomes blurry.

Sometimes we lose our vision, both the "why" of *what we do* and the "how" we *see* life. We forget why we work and we don't know how to interpret why it matters.

To simplify, the *why* of what we do is the gospel. And the *how* of what we do is the gospel. Let's explore the *why* and *how* behind the difference the gospel makes in our lives.

The Gospel Is Perfect Vision

The gospel is a message about a person; the Truth of what Jesus has done for us. God the Son came down to earth. Sinless, He bore our sin on the cross, dying in our place. The gospel isn't a force, a power to wield. The gospel is the truth of Jesus as God, our Savior and King.

To believe Jesus is Lord, and in His atoning sacrifice for your sin, is salvation. Saved from hell and from sin, your heart has been transformed by His miraculous grace! There is nothing you can do to merit this holy love. This radical love is from Christ Himself. He rose from death and ascended to the Father. He sent the Holy Spirit to dwell within you, sister, so that your heart and life will continue to bring glory to Him. This amazing gospel changes everything about your heart and your future. Your destiny is with Him, loved and cherished by God. It seems too good to be true, yet it is true! He has promised these things to us.

If we believe the gospel, then its truth seeps deep into our soul, remaking us. We love Jesus, accept this gospel-gift, and become changed as a result. The gospel redeems our lives! We are reborn, renewed, and redeemed. Our vision may have been good—maybe even moral before—but now the gospel has purified our vision for His purposes, not our own. Our self-significant dreams get re-routed to godly ambition: to worship Jesus in all we do.

The truth of the gospel frees us. We are defined by His grace. God lavishes His love on us. Living out the gospel and embracing the grace of God is a daily belief and action. In myself, at times, I don't want to get up and do the work of serving my family. Selfishly, I would rather be sitting on a beach somewhere reading, alone. But, because I have been rescued, redeemed, and continually pursued by an amazing God, my desires continue to change. Because Jesus has given me His righteousness, I want to worship Him in my daily actions, thoughts, deeds, relationships, and especially my desires. He has given me a new heart and new desires. I want to worship Jesus in and through my work. Not so I can boast, but so that Jesus looks good.

> [H]e chose us in him before the foundation of the world, that we should be holy and blameless before him. In love he predestined us for adoption as sons through Jesus Christ, according to the purpose of his will, to the praise of his glorious grace, with which he has blessed us in the Beloved. In him we have redemption through his blood, the forgiveness of our trespasses, according to the riches of his grace, which he lavished upon us, in all wisdom and insight. (Eph. 1:4-8)

The Gospel Isn't Rule Following

As we embrace the truth of the gospel, the Holy Spirit changes our desires, thoughts, and motives. Grace is given, allowing us to see Jesus more clearly. Yet, we still struggle. We lose our grip on the gospel and how it motivates us, down deep.

For me, I can get caught up in rule following, thinking that I can earn God's love. I start to think that if I obey Him, if I work hard—He might approve of me. However, God sees *Jesus'* obedience and approves of me. His affection and my salvation are given because of *Jesus'* perfect obedience. My rule following gets me nowhere with God. Miraculously, His grace covers my life—inviting my worship. This is good news!

> And you were dead in the trespasses and sins...and were by nature children of wrath, like the rest of mankind. But God, being rich in mercy, because of the great love with which he loved us, even when we were dead in our trespasses, made us alive together with Christ—by grace you have been saved. (Eph. 2:1, 3-5)

This means we are free to live as He created us ... alive in His Grace! We don't have to choose bondage to our works or our sins.

STRUGGLING TO SEE

Even in the best of times, vision is still blurry. Most days, work pressures and temptations to grumble lure us. We fight selfishness and tell ourselves to work hard and that "we can do it!" The heart battle goes on, and we barely make it to the end of the day with peace and contentment. The struggle to see Jesus in the mundane is a daily fight.

Forgetful and visionless, we've missed the why of our work. We often work disconnected from the meaning, purpose, and vision of why we work.

We work for Jesus, remember? Not that we earn anything by it, but our aim is for Him. God is watching and is with us, guiding our steps, hearts, and lives. His grace fuels us. When we work worshipfully, our hands are busy, our hearts are engaged, and our eyes are fixed on Jesus.

> Therefore, since we are surrounded by such a great cloud of witnesses, let us throw off everything that hinders and the sin that so easily entangles. And let us run with perseverance the race marked out for us, fixing our eyes on Jesus, the pioneer and perfecter of faith. For the joy set before him he endured the cross, scorning its shame, and sat down at the right hand of the throne of God. Consider him who endured such opposition from sinners, so that you will not grow weary and lose heart. (Heb. 12:1-2, NIV)

THE GOSPEL IS OURS EVERY DAY

Gospel language is all around us, and if you have grown up in the church, you are used to these words. You may have even tuned me out, hoping that I will let you in on the *real* secret for how to apply the gospel to daily life. To totally frustrate you, I won't tell you anything you haven't probably already heard one hundred times. But, I invite you to listen differently. You are reading this in the hope that your belief in Jesus will transform your heart more deeply, and the joy that comes from knowing Him will flow into your daily life, right? Then, challenge yourself. Ask "why?" Pray that the Holy Spirit will expose unbelief and inspire belief.

- Why does the cross of Jesus change the way you do your dishes?

- How does knowing Jesus affect your relationships?

- Does His love really change your dreams?

- Have you forgotten how your first love (Jesus) has healed your wounds? This same Lord is with you as you drive your kids to school.

- Does knowing Jesus change the way you view politics, the earth, your past?

- Have you been changed by this good news—the gospel?

- Was His giving His life for yours enough to re-focus your eyes on Him?

- Why wouldn't this Holy Love change your passions and reason for living?

My plea to you, dear sister, is that your vision would be on Jesus. That your eyes, as in Hebrews 12, would be fixed on Him, the author and perfecter of your faith, not on your overwhelming amount of work or your circumstance. But, in facing those things, understand that your diligence and accomplishments are because of Jesus. Your heart is aware of your constant need for Him and your aim is to worship Him in your thoughts and actions.

It is easy to get distracted or forgetful. Because of sin, our vision gets cloudy from time to time. Thankfully, He gives us grace. As we look to Him in our work, our vision gets clearer. Our grace-giving Father, God, doesn't give us a bad report as a result of our lack of vision. He gently invites us back to worship, reminding us that in Jesus, our worship is perfect.

The list below describes some of the differences between how we work when we understand the "why" and how we work when we are forgetful of God's grace:

Lost Vision—just work	Vision-filled heart— work as worship
Task list held tightly, numb heart—dutiful about tasks but disengaged emotionally	Task list held loosely, sensitive heart—ready to respond as God leads
Demands for your time cause you to grumble and be resentful about serving others	You give your attention willingly, finding joy in loving others
Busy schedule, frustrated and chaotic	Schedule shaped by discernment, priorities, prayer; you are striving for peace
Dirty laundry piles, procrastination	Hard work; you are humbled by the difficulty and physical demands
Self-focused, wanting appreciation for work	Others-focused, knowing that your reward is God Himself
Stressed and bearing your own burdens—you don't ask for help	Acknowledging you can't do anything apart from God and the help of your family and friends

Buried under paperwork and expectations—fearful you won't get through it	Confident that God is with you and He gives you constant strength
Clean house, finished task list—forgetful of God's presence	Thankful for productivity, knowing that grace gave you what you needed

Lest we forget, I want to remind us again that the only way to have a godly, redeemed vision is by His *grace*. Sin infiltrates our vision, and because of God's grace, our vision gets corrected. As we look at Jesus, He corrects our sight. We start interpreting all of life through this grace. It is quite miraculous, actually. We can't take a "vision pill" or get fired up by some vision sermon and have it leave a lasting effect on our souls. The gospel isn't a formula or a how-to. The only way to live out a gospel vision is to worshipfully accept His gift of grace. And this takes daily practice with each decision we make, it's not a one-time choice.

Furthermore, this transformational grace corrects our vision, giving us Jesus' eyes. Though sin is still a shadow on our sight, believing the gospel gives us new and holy lenses. We can trust Jesus to redeem our heart's vision. And we need the gospel to live in this transformed state every single day.

If we want to live grace-filled lives of love and purpose, our vision must be on Jesus: seeing and savoring His grace, enjoying Him, and worshiping Him in all that we do.

> God created me—and you—to live with a single, all-embracing, all-transforming passion—namely, a passion to glorify God by enjoying and displaying his supreme excellence in all the spheres of life. —John Piper[2]

---

2   Piper, John. *Don't Waste Your Life* (Wheaton, IL: Crossway Publishers, 2003), p. 31.

REFLECTION QUESTIONS

1. How does the gospel change your daily life?

2. Are you forgetful or apathetic about God's presence? How might you remember His affection for you?

3. Are you prone to work for God's love?

4. What does a godly vision look like in your daily life as you serve Jesus?

5. Are you joyful? Why?

6. When you are depressed, are you aware of God?

Chapter 16

We are His Workmanship

God created us for this: to live our lives in a way that makes him look more like the greatness and the beauty and the infinite worth that he really is. This is what it means to be created in the image of God.

John Piper[1]

We work every day. Unless you live on a beach somewhere and money just falls from the sky, working is necessary for survival. Yet, many of us don't ask the "why" questions of our daily human routines, such as work.

One reason we work is because we were made in God's image to reflect Him. He is a worker. He created work. And we demonstrate His grace in work (in our hearts and actions) while we work. Our labor actually matters! More than a paycheck or fulfilled dream, we get to represent the God of the universe when we work. Can you believe that?

Furthermore, our work's purpose is to give God glory. Our work is a response to His. Let's explore how our work is worship!

---

1   Piper, John. *Don't Waste Your Life* (Wheaton, IL: Crossway Publishers, 2003), p. 32.

GOD IS A WORKER

We see in Genesis 1 and 2 Creator God.

> And on the seventh day God finished his work that he had
> done, and he rested on the seventh day from all his work that
> he had done. (Gen. 2:2)

Work is ancient. God Himself created work, and He Himself
works. This characteristic of God is evident throughout Scripture.
As He created all things, He also works all things to His glory.
Work is from God, for God.

Another part of God's work is that He holds all things
together.

> And he is before all things, and in him all things hold together.
> (Col. 1:17)

And while He is holding the cosmos together, He is also holding
us close—His kids. His work is personal and purposed in His
affection for His children.

> For you formed my inward parts; you knitted me together
> in my mother's womb. I praise you, for I am fearfully and
> wonderfully made. Wonderful are your works; my soul knows
> it very well. My frame was not hidden from you, when I was
> being made in secret, intricately woven in the depths of the
> earth. (Ps. 139:13-15)

GOD IS OUR WORKING FATHER

Growing up without a father, my view of "dad" was full of
uncertain and painful experiences with men who pledged short-
term love to my mother, me, and my sister. My desire for a dad
subsided as time went on. As I grew in Christ, my understanding
of God the Father became more theological than emotional.
The thoughts of God being a dad, paying attention to my heart
and life, at first seemed foreign; but over time, I have started to
cling to my Father God like a toddler pulling on her daddy's leg,
trusting that His goodness is real and He will always pick me up.

God is faithfully correcting my view of "Father," not by changing my earthly circumstances first, but by teaching me a biblical understanding of Him as Father. All of my other relationships fall short of His perfect love.

God is paying attention to us and is working on us with detailed love—like a perfect Father.

HE IS A FAITHFUL DAD AND DELIGHTS IN HIS KIDS

> Therefore, my beloved, as you have always obeyed, so now not only as in my presence but now much more in my absence, work out your own salvation with fear and trembling, for it is God who works in you, both to will and to work for his good pleasure. (Phil. 2:12-14)

God Who Works in You

As believers, we are fearful (out of respect, honor, humility) at God's presence, and God is actively paying attention. He is taking notes on us, thinking about us, knowing us, arranging things for us, and lovingly guiding the whole universe to work according to His plan for each of us.

Can you believe that the same Lord who placed the stars in the sky and imagined and created every living creature is with us, watching us, loving us, and working things out for us? I am in awe at the hugeness yet personal-ness of our God! I love that God works for His own satisfaction, glory, and pleasure. He is holy in His pursuit of His own glory.

And Jesus is praying for us.

- To keep us from evil: "I do not ask that you take them out of the world, but that you keep them from the evil one" (John 17:15).

- To make us holy: "Sanctify them in the truth; your word is truth" (John 17:17).

- To see glory: "Father, I desire that they also, whom you have given me, may be with me where I am, to see my glory

that you have given me because you loved me before the
foundation of the world" (John 17:24).

The other day, I explained to my sons that God is thinking about
them and working on their hearts. For an example, I shared how
I have a "momma" journal that records shepherding ideas for my
children individually, what is going on in their lives, and how
to encourage, serve, protect them. I could see that the boys felt
loved and honored by this journal. I explained that the journal
entries are a small picture of the Great Shepherd's detailed
thoughtfulness. He is all-knowing, all-powerful, and perfect. He
never slumbers or sleeps (Ps. 121).

For His Good Pleasure

I sit here and try to picture God's pleasure. What does that look
like? Is He laughing in delight in heaven? Is His pleasure like
sunshine rays coming through clouds? What does it look like
for God to will and to work for His good pleasure? I know but
a small piece of what perfect pleasure beyond sin's stain in my
heart feels like. Our pleasure is momentary, but God's pleasure
must be more majestic and beautiful than the most glorious
sunset I've ever seen. If I dwell on what God's pleasure might
be like, it is quite breath-taking to read how His pleasure is felt
when He thinks of us, His children.

> The LORD takes pleasure in those who fear him, in those who
> hope in his steadfast love. (Ps. 147:11)

I love that God delights in His work and that I am one of the
works He delights in, knows, loves personally, and works things
out in, for my good, ultimately giving Himself glory.

I do not work on my own. It is God willing and working
in His magnificent power and attention to the details of my
heart. As my heart worships God-replacements (idols) less over
time, I am at a place where that "fear and trembling" is more
frequent, my heart is full of adoration, and I am completely
awestruck!

We work out our salvation with fear of the Lord, as He delights in us, His kids. "Being delighted in" may seem like a strange and foreign concept to you, one that feels scary, yet wonderful. Our God says He delights in His children. We bring Him joy!

His perfect work proves we can always trust His attention to detail. Our work is mostly frustrated labor with some joys sparkling through. When we are struggling in our work, we can look to the best worker, the one who carries us through the difficulty.

God, as a worker and a Holy Dad, delights in Himself and us. We know that because of our sinful nature and the curse (Gen. 2), our work is often burdensome. As we look to our Father, what is our response? How can our work be worship? Can our mundane and significant tasks actually reflect the holiness of God?

GOD THE WORKING FATHER VERSUS OUR WORK

- His work is never stressful; our work is always burdened in some way.

- He never sleeps; we must sleep.

- He never gets weak or weary; we are weak and weary.

- He is everywhere at the same time; we never seem to have enough time.

- He never gives up on His mission; we often give up when it gets tough.

- He makes Himself happy; if and when we are done, we are happy.

- He delights in His kids; we grumble about our work.

- He never fights with His co-workers; we have relational strain.

- He always gets His way; we struggle to submit to God's will.

- His plans are always perfect; our plans always include mistakes.

- His sovereign love is constantly given; we easily forget to show love in our work.

WORK IS FOR GOD

> For we are God's fellow workers. You are God's field, God's
> building. (1 Cor. 3:9)

We work because we were made in the image of God. God gets glory for Himself as we reflect some aspect of who He is. One way we demonstrate His goodness is through the role of working.

While God does not "need" us to accomplish His work, we get to help Him do his work. As we work, we bear His image.

JESUS WORKED

> This is a wonderful thing, that the Savior of the world, and the
> King above kings, was not ashamed to labor; yea and to use so
> simple an occupation. Here he did sanctify all manner of all
> occupations.—Hugh Latimer[2]

Jesus worked as a carpenter for possibly as many as twenty years before He began His public ministry (Mark 6:3). When the Jews confronted Jesus about the Sabbath, Jesus said to them, "My Father is always at his work to this very day, and I too am working" (John 5:17, NIV). Jesus' listeners didn't understand who Jesus really was. Later on in John 5:36, He further explains, "But the testimony that I have is greater than that of John. For the works that the Father has given me to accomplish, the very works that I am doing, bear witness about me that the Father has sent me." Jesus was doing the Father's work—perfectly.

WE ARE GOD'S WORK

> For we are his workmanship, created in Christ Jesus for good
> works, which God prepared beforehand, that we should walk
> in them. (Eph. 2:10)

As God's children, we are His work. Seeking us out, He begins a good work in our hearts. Attentive and passionate, His fatherly

---

2   Hugh Latimer, quoted in Leland Ryken, *Worldly Saints* (Grand Rapids, MI:
     Zondervan Publishers, 1986), p. 25.

care continues to work through our hearts, preparing us for good works and becoming more satisfied in His love.

He is not a cold, absent boss always giving us a workload. Instead, he works in our hearts, mightily inviting us to experience His miraculous love. He saves us from sin and gives us grace every day to walk closely with Him. No, His management over our lives isn't like anything we've experienced from an earthly manager or even from our fathers.

> And I am sure of this, that he who began a good work in you will bring it to completion at the day of Jesus Christ. (Phil. 1:6)

We are His work, and He gives us work to do, because He loves us.

GOD IS THE DECISIVE WORKER

> Therefore, my beloved, as you have always obeyed, so now, not only as in my presence but much more in my absence, work out your own salvation with fear and trembling, for it is God who works in you, both to will and to work for his good pleasure. (Phil. 2:12-13)

As I am doing my "works, good deeds, labor," God is, by the Holy Spirit, moving my hands, and in my heart, showing me His grace. His glory is revealed in the duties, works, and righteousness because of Jesus. I have this image in my head of a misty glory rising off my body because of Jesus, and God is at work to receive it. That glory is radiant and it is *all* His!

OUR WORK AS WORSHIP

> I do not think we should ever work until we learn to worship. A worshiper can work with eternal quality in his work but a worker who does not worship is only piling up wood, hay and stubble for the time when God sets the world on fire. God wants worshipers before He wants workers…Our work is only acceptable to God if our worship is acceptable.—A.W. Tozer[3]

---

3   Tozer, A.W. *The Purpose of Man* (Ventura, CA: Regal Books, 2009), p. 95.

When we truly believe God is a good dad who delights in us and is showing us how to demonstrate His grace, often through work, we start to scratch the surface of worship.

Work is worship when:

- We embrace God as the perfect Father, working in us, His children.

- Our hearts fear Him, acknowledging His power at work in us.

- Our posture is meek, acknowledging our weakness and our need for His grace.

- We have joy, knowing our God is delighting in us as we work, engaged in what He has called us to do.

- Our lives radiate redemption, claiming no strength in ourselves, but boasting in what Jesus has done for us.

REFLECTION QUESTIONS

1. Do you struggle with relating to God as Father?

2. How would your work change if you saw God as faithful, holy, and affectionate in His attention to your heart as you work?

3. How does the fact that God delights in you feel?

4. When you work, do you find that you forget God's tender care for you?

CHAPTER 17

Prayer brings Peace

Therefore, since we have been justified by faith, we have peace with God through our Lord Jesus Christ.

(Rom. 5:1)

JESUS IS OUR PEACE

Jesus gives us peace by giving us Himself. Knowing Jesus brings life and daily peace, not based on circumstances, but on being loved by God. Jesus reaches into our lives and saves us from sin and the anxiety in our hearts.

> Peace I leave with you; my peace I give to you. Not as the world gives do I give to you. Let not your hearts be troubled, neither let them be afraid. (John 14:27)

This peace isn't simple peace. It is the simplicity on the far side of complexity. The complexity? Many layers of fears, sin, and our confusing pasts that leave us wounded, numb, and feeling erratic. Jesus' peace is given in simply knowing Him, yet we resist Him. Striving for peace, we often miss true peace—Jesus.

This peace is relationally real and beautiful. Experiencing it causes us to breathe in deeply the truth that God has our hearts and lives in His hands, carefully caring for us. Nothing surprises Him. He is glorified as we hand Him our struggles, trusting Him to give us peace.

You keep him in perfect peace whose mind is stayed on you, because he trusts in you. (Isa. 26:3)

YET, WE STILL FEEL ANXIOUS

The opposite of peace is anxiety, chaos, conflict, and numbness. When we are under stress, we are tempted toward fear and anxiety.

For me, relational conflict, financial strain, even a change in plans, can stir up anxiety. Any event that would tempt me to doubt God's goodness is an opportunity to fight fear, and to fight for fear of the Lord. But, again, it is the simple fight through the complexity of drama that brings simple faith.

One might religiously say, "Oh, *just* trust God." When we hear this, it usually feels cold and gross because it lacks the dignity and respect for those of us who are in the anxiety-ridden situation. We want to encourage one another to trust God in a way that shows our care and patience.

To *trust God* is to *expect good* from Him. Yet, when we are struggling, it is a constant temptation to doubt His goodness.

Walking through the drama of a difficult circumstance with Jesus means we constantly fight unbelief, resisting the temptation to think God is far from us and isn't loving us. We walk, growing in our trust of Him, expecting Him to carry us through the difficulty.

The opposite of an anxious heart is a peaceful heart. When we aren't giving our worries over to the Lord, we become anxious. Trusting Him enables us to take deep, calm breaths, believing that nothing is out of His care. When we trust Him, we know that His goodness always wins out eventually and replaces anxiety.

Worry, fretting, and allowing our minds to linger on the "what ifs" is a real experience for everyone at various times. As we are tempted to lose hope in God, we easily become fearful.

Granted, there are experiences that are truly ridden with anxiety. The effects of sin—in the world and to us, personally—are devastating. To be anxious over a real trial is understandable. Death, abuse, or pain brings raw angst as the effects touch deep parts of our soul. Living in light of those experiences reveals our need. If you have anxiety as part of your journey in processing something very difficult, it may be that you are still fighting for your faith. God is patient and compassionate. He wants you to continually, prayerfully give Him your burdens and ask Him for wisdom as you process your pain.

WORRY INSTEAD OF WORSHIP

Sometimes, we accept our weakness and become meek, worshiping Christ in our need. Other times, we believe there is life in the worry. Wooed by the familiarity of chaos, peace seems unreachable.

Anxiety never brings life; it only encourages unbelief. The only way to make sense of our daily mess is to come to God in prayer, believing that He is loving us.

> Do not be anxious about anything, but in everything by prayer and supplication with thanksgiving let your requests be made known to God. And the peace of God, which surpasses all understanding, will guard your hearts and your minds in Christ Jesus. (Phil. 4:6-7)

Sometimes, attempts at creating our own peace through false comforts bring momentary relief to our anxiety. For me, when life throws me a curve ball, my first reaction is worry, not prayer. And often, I try to solve my anxiety with planning, my go-to quick fix for the chaos.

TRYING TO GET PEACE THROUGH PLANNING?

Three years ago, my husband and I began home-schooling our four children. Months before starting the school year, I set out to plan our academic success. As I researched, I found myself surrounded with insurmountable mountains of educational philosophies, both in principle and in method. Making wise decisions for our family seemed impossible. I was overwhelmed by the burden and weight of the decisions. I was humbled by my need for clarity and peace. How could I ever feel confident of what we chose to teach our children? Worry enveloped me. The chaos of indecision exposed my need for control. And, usually when I feel out of control, I scramble for it. I demand order.

Eventually, I realized I couldn't get control through "my plan." I couldn't possibly navigate through the crowded options. There was no way my heart would find peace through planning, because I couldn't even imagine the plan. I needed another route to peace in my soul.

I had to pray.

Prayer for me is hit-and-miss, inconsistent. I love my time with the Lord and enjoy His presence throughout my days (when I actually acknowledge Him). However, my ambitious heart seeks to conquer the day, and I often neglect sweet dependence on the Holy Spirit. As the home-schooling walls started closing in on me, I felt out of control. The urge to plan, schedule, and make decisions became like a force tempting me to find my own peace, and quick! I was far from thinking about Paul's words here:

> And let the peace of Christ rule in your hearts, to which indeed you were called in one body. And be thankful. (Col. 3:15)

And…I didn't plan. For months. If you knew me, you would have been surprised. Not planning, for me, revealed that God was *fully* after my heart, wanting me to find restful peace in Him, alone. God wanted me to pray and receive peace to believe that He would guide, provide wisdom, and calm my anxious heart. As He comforted me, joy and peace followed. I began to experience a deep sense that God was in control and was moving my mind, hands, and heart to the good He wanted for me and my family. My heart changed as God convicted me of fear and I let go of planning and instead prayed. The plan did come, but it came as an after-thought, a new experience for me. I didn't get peace through my plan, first.

Peace with God happened through prayer, not my plan.

Prayer isn't a formula, and being a "good planner" isn't the goal. Only in Christ do I find the peace that sustains me. Prayer is me saying to God, "*You* know me, and I want to know *you*, walk in *your* presence, and depend on *you* with every step, especially in my plans."

PLANNING BRINGS SOME PEACE (CIRCUMSTANTIALLY), BUT PRAYER BRINGS REAL PEACE

For the chaotic details of our lives, we try to make sense of the chaos by either planning (controlling) or allowing anxiety to reign in our hearts. Planning can be worshipful, but it can also easily be a quick fix to my anxiety.

Ok. What does this look like in everyday life? Stress erupts. Tempts us to doubt and worry. We are now at an intersection of belief or unbelief. Is God still with us? Are we trusting Him? Is He still loving us? Sometimes, we turn left toward anxiety, embracing unbelief. Sometimes, we turn right toward peace, embracing belief that God is good and provides peace. Faith drives us closer to Him, and prayer acknowledges belief that Jesus provides peace. The Holy Spirit supplies peace as we trust.

For me, planning brings artificial peace. For you? It might be food that numbs your heart to the drama in your soul. It may be disconnecting relationally from whoever is the source of your drama or anxiety. It may be that fear freezes you, and you are still functioning physically, but your heart is cold and isolated. Whatever your response to drama and chaos, pain and toil, the first step out of it is to recognize your godless response. How is your response to pain rejecting the satisfying comfort of the only lasting refuge?

I am proposing that true peace is knowing God. As we grow in the fear of the Lord, our fears of this life begin to subside and we experience more frequent deep peace. Prayer expresses our acknowledgement that God is at work in our hearts and that we trust Him.

While we are in a moment of relative calm, we need to humble ourselves and admit that we are easily tempted to worry in the midst of chaos and that we often desire to get control. We are easily pursued by the temptation to hide in false comforts instead of in God's true comfort. As we humble ourselves, our hearts become meek and worshipful. The apostle Peter says it this way:

> Humble yourselves, therefore, under the mighty hand of God so that at the proper time he may exalt you, casting all your anxieties on him, because he cares for you. (1 Pet. 5:6-7)

How Prayer Brings Peace to Our Hearts

When we believe God is good, we actively replace fear, anxiety, and worry with belief, trust, and relationship with Jesus. It is a fight! Yet, it is a fight that Jesus has already won on the cross. It is our privilege to accept that, especially when the fight has worn us down and we feel unable to fight anymore. We cry out right in the middle of our worry, "God, help me believe that you are fighting for me. You are my peace."

> But now in Christ Jesus you who once were far off have been brought near by the blood of Christ. For he himself is our peace, who has made us both one and has broken down in his flesh the dividing wall of hostility. (Eph. 2:13-14)

If Jesus is our peace, how do we actually live that out daily?

Prayer Acknowledges His Presence, His Power, and His Purpose at Work in Us

Prayer is an acknowledgement of our dependence on God.

We know we can't do anything apart from the grace of God, yet we go through our days not depending on Him. When we stop for a moment to acknowledge God, we are praying; whether we speak words or not, we are aware of His presence.

Prayer is talking with and enjoying our Father, Savior, Helper.

Isn't it amazing that we can talk to God? He is listening and loving us constantly! In worship, we bring our attention to Him, aware of His love; we pray to Him. He is our attentive Father, both powerfully and tenderly hearing our cries, and points of gratitude.

> Then they cried to the Lord in their trouble, and he delivered them from their distress. He made the storm be still, and the

waves of the sea were hushed. Then they were glad that the
waters were quiet, and he brought them to their desired haven.
(Ps. 107:28-30)

PRAYER IS PRODUCTIVE

The prayer of a righteous person has great power as it is
working. (James 5:16b)

Because our faith engages a powerful God, our prayers are heard
powerfully. God listens to His children. As the Spirit comforts,
guides, and convicts, we are productive in our faith, growing
ever closer to Jesus.

PRAYER INVITES YOU TO LISTEN TO GOD

Life has a way of drowning out the voice of the Lord. We strain
to hear Him, yet our technology, screaming, schedules, and other
voices are much louder than the holy voice we really want to
hear. When we pray, listening to God's voice is the priority. We
choose Him over distractions. Like a needy child, we come to
our daddy wanting His attention, answers to our questions, and
just to sit with Him—enjoying Him.

PRAYER ENJOYS GOD'S PRESENCE

Evening and morning and at noon I utter my complaint and
moan, and he hears my voice. (Ps. 55:17)

When do you seek God's presence in prayer? If we are in
relationship with God, we have an everyday, constant awareness
of His nearness. Because we have His Spirit dwelling within
us, we have non-stop access to our Father. My pastor often says
that we pray "to the Father, through the Son, by the Spirit" (see
Eph. 2:18). We pray, knowing He is with us. His presence is
certain.

Reflection Questions

1. When do you find you are most prone to reach out to God in prayer?

2. When was the last time you found yourself really enjoying God's company as you prayed?

3. If you truly believed God's presence was certain, how would that change the frequency and manner in which you pray?

Chapter 18

Rest for the Weary

And on the seventh day God finished his work that
he had done, and he rested on the seventh day from
all his work that he had done.

(Gen. 2:2)

The other side of work is rest.

God Rested

We are finite creatures, unlike our infinite God. After six days of work, He rested. He didn't need rest, yet He rested—for an entire day! His rest wasn't like ours; He wasn't weak or tired. He didn't need to rest just to make it through to the next crazy, busy week.

Rest is more than sleep; it is restoration. We are mind, body, soul. Our bodies often rest first, but do our minds and souls?

God Wants Us To Rest

I usually don't rest well. It is partly my life as a wife and mother of young children. The very nature of my days doesn't bring rest.

I naturally work hard, stay busy, and rarely stop to recharge, or pause work to rest. Work is my default, and rest is more difficult. I work until I "need" to rest. I work to the point of exhaustion.

Rest is often more of a necessity instead of a delight in disciplined restoration for our bodies and hearts. God invites us to rest, not as an optional survival method, but as worship.

How many of us, when we do rest, take the moments to enjoy God? Or enjoy that our busyness is stilled and our souls find satisfaction in the refreshment of God? And when we experience this soul rest, do we regret not resting more often?

Exactly.

That is why God established the Sabbath—to give us weekly opportunity to worship Him with disciplined rest. Our bodies slow down long enough for our minds to hear the Lord, enjoy Him, and be renewed.

We can rest because we can trust God to take care of us.

> He will not let your foot be moved; he who keeps you will not slumber. Behold, he who keeps Israel will neither slumber nor sleep. The LORD is your keeper; the LORD is your shade on your right hand. The sun shall not strike you by day, nor the moon by night. The LORD will keep you from all evil; he will keep your life. The LORD will keep your going out and your coming in from this time forth and forevermore. (Ps. 121:3-8)

Our God does not sleep; He is constantly aware and watchful. We can rest because our Lord cares for us. I don't know about you, but that makes me want to calm down, take deep breaths, feel the warmth of my Savior's protection around me, and rest.

> Come to me, all who labor and are heavy laden, and I will give you rest. Take my yoke upon you, and learn from me, for I am gentle and lowly in heart, and you will find rest for your souls. For my yoke is easy, and my burden is light. (Matt. 11:28-30)

TWO KINDS OF REST

Sabbath Rest

The idea of the Sabbath is to purposely plan on breaking from our work to turn our attention, our hearts, toward Jesus. While I am not recommending a legalistic view of the Sabbath day in our lives, the blessing of having a Sabbath is very practical. Most of us don't take spontaneous vacations; those are planned far in advance. To truly take a break from our work requires planning. Practicing a Sabbath usually requires intentional planning to shift our focus away from our task list, to listen to the Lord, and to enjoy Him in a more focused way.

This rest is planned, and its purpose is to give us a break from labor. God designed the Sabbath for His children to pause from work to experience rest. Sabbath is a gift of grace, as we ask God for the discipline to take a Sabbath rest. Our bodies get tired; we need to take breaks. Physical rest can re-energize us and provide an opportunity for a deeper rest—soul rest.

Be still and know that I am God. (Ps. 46:10).

Soul Rest

There is also rest that can be experienced in our hearts, even as we work. This kind of rest is still purposeful and turns our hearts' attention on Jesus. I have a few friends that love to garden. They thoroughly enjoy tilling soil, planting, and pulling weeds. They delight in their work, breaking into a sweat as they labor, and they find it worshipful, because their hearts are at rest. For me, when I crochet, do dishes, or even write, I am physically working and feeling productive, but because I am still while doing it, I have tender moments of focus on Jesus.

Our bodies do not have to stop working to enjoy communion with God. Because we can be in constant communion with the Holy Spirit, our hearts can enjoy God even as we work.

For I will satisfy the weary soul, and every languishing soul I will replenish. (Jer. 31:25)

SETTLING FOR THE WRONG KIND OF REST

Rest is meant for restoration and can be worshipful. Often, we think that a day off from our labor will do the trick. We know that both physical and soul rest in Christ restore us. Yet, too often we settle for false rest.

We often wait until we are completely desperate for rest before we rest.

For me, when I am at the point of exhaustion and am spiraling down into grumbling, I often choose the wrong road of false hopes, false rest. Desperate, I make foolish "if only" statements.

"If only we had more money."

"If only I had a date night with my husband."

"If only I could get my house really clean."

"If only I had alone time."

"If only I could sleep more."

Feeling inadequate and out of control of any number of life stresses, I feel small and weak. My soul rest is connected to my belief or unbelief. Instead of being humbled, I tend to reject the discomfort of my need and become prideful. I demand control, believing that if I regain it, I will be restored. My wandering, grumbling heart searches for some end to my familiar fatigue.

If I am anxious, it is likely that my heart is not restful. When stress strikes, I can only experience rest if I lay anxiety at Jesus' feet.

Jesus Is Our Peaceful Rest

If Only I'd Hope in God

Here's what my "if only's" tell God: what He has given me, in some moment, is not good, and I'll hope when the conditions are met, not at all times, in Him. Exhaustion is an occasion to demand, to grumble—or to find hope in God, again.

Recently, frazzled and mumbling "if only's," I opened Psalm 23 with a chaotic heart, throwing a silent fit before God: *OK, fine! I will read my Bible. I know that is what you want.* The Psalm surprised and confronted me with words that exposed the sin of my misplaced hope.

I foolishly believed I could escape exhaustion by submitting my "if only" list for God to fulfill—totally missing that He is my greatest restoration. If God would just give me sleep or alone time, then I would be OK. But God, relentless in His faithfulness, reveals all the measly hopes of my soul being restored, because nothing actually satisfies a craving heart more than Jesus. When I'm tired, weak, and tempted, He gently leads me to Himself.

He leads me beside still waters. He restores my soul (Ps. 23:2).

It is He who restores my soul. All of the alone time and money in the world can't compare to God's presence. Clean homes and date nights are blessings, but are meaningless unless God's presence is enjoyed. Sure, sleep boosts my weary body, but my soul is only restored by Jesus.

GOD IS THE MEANS—AND THE END

It's not magic, though. I don't just limp toward God's word, open it, and magically return to my joyful and rested self. Sometimes, it is a tooth-and-nail fight to resist grumbling and doubt in my heart.

To let God restore us is to want *Him* more than the effects of being restored. Get that? It's like the difference between wanting coffee merely for an energy boost, rather than for its taste and aroma, too.

God is not just the way to get rest. He is both the way and the destination for our soul rest.

A QUIET, PEACEFUL JOY

As we submit our hearts to Jesus, weariness becomes a quiet joy. Our gloom turns to peace. God's word gives us hope as our weakness is laid at His feet; He tells us His power is made perfect in our weakness (2 Cor. 12:9).

It's amazing. Wearily, we can come to the Father, and He always meets us, comforts us, speaks to us, and holds us close. The only true rest is in God alone, and there's no "if" to it; He always satisfies.

REFLECTION QUESTIONS

1. When do you rest?

2. What excuses do you typically make to avoid taking soul rest?

3. When you rest, do you aim for rest in God?

4. How could soul rest impact your physical rest? How are the two related?

PART FOUR:

Heart Change

CHAPTER 19

From Busy-Body to Busy Bee

Besides, they get into the habit of being idle and going about from house to house. And not only do they become idlers, but also gossips and busybodies, saying things they ought not to.

(1 Tim. 5:13).

Busy-body. Those words are power-packed with negative associations, right? The "town gossip lady" picture in my head is not the *busy at home lady*, but instead is the woman who knows facts about others' lives and is stocked with random trivia. Instead of quietly working in her home and for her family, the busy-body is more concerned with the actions, thoughts, and juicy tidbits of others.

I certainly never thought *I* was gossipy, idle, lazy, or randomly wandering about my day, looking for someone or something to scratch an itch in my heart.

A New Kind of Busy-Body
But wait. As it turns out, the Internet is my "town" to meander through. I hadn't identified much with this particular sin until God gently showed me that I had been going "from house to

house" or "website to website," seeking something. Information, book reviews, blogs, Facebook, email, all eating up my time and seducing my attention.

To ignore this comparison is to choose blindness—blindness to the fact that I'm tempted to neglect the people and gifts God has called me to pay attention to. Sin is giving in to the temptation to *busy-body* by giving my attention to worthless and sometimes meaningless information that swirls around in my head, taking up mind and heart space that should be occupied by prayers and purpose.

When was the last time you found yourself going from house to house being idle? Or, perhaps, calling or texting too many friends in one day just to chat? Does boredom lure you to busy-bodying? What do you gain by knowing more stuff? When does being curious distract your heart from what God wants you to focus on?

The sin of the busy-body often arises when desires are disappointed and we either demand or settle for the pleasure of knowing others' business. Instead of being connected relationally to God and people, we slip into false intimacy and gather knowledge that doesn't grow us, but instead wastes time. Like greed or lust, busy-bodying is a thirst for more. We are saying to God that He doesn't satisfy our hearts.

BUSY-BODIES CAN REPENT

We don't just need more "balance" in our lives; we need to repent of misplaced desires, laziness, and lustful curiosity. Repentance does not always mean we have to adopt the opposite behavior. The potential pitfalls of being online too much doesn't mean that social networking is bad, or that email, Internet, and helpful websites are inherently sinful. As much as legalism lures me, I believe repentance doesn't just mean making new rules for myself here, but instead involves being sensitive to the Holy Spirit, moment by moment, day by day, with my time and attention. I grieve the time I have wasted by not making thoughtful choices. Thankfully, God always gives perfect attention to His children. He is faithful, and I am not. I get to respond to Jesus with gratitude for His grace and to grow in wisdom by stewarding my attention and time.

Practically, this means I set prayerful boundaries on time spent on websites. I choose appropriate times to give attention to it, choosing times where relationships aren't ignored. Stewarding my time means seeing "Internet time" as a resource to be used with wisdom and as worship to Jesus.

Internet busy-bodying is really just another form of laziness and escapism. The truth is: I will never perfectly steward my time and attention, but God does pay close and perfect attention. My heart is humbled by the struggle, and I'm eager to see redemption. By God's lavish grace, I can steward my time with wisdom enabled by the Holy Spirit. Knowing Jesus is true satisfaction for my curious heart.

And There Are Busy Bees

If a busy-body is one who cares too much about other people's lives, a busy bee is an industrious woman that is probably too busy with her own life and family to peer into others'. The busy-body can become a busy bee when her heart is turned from other people to her own home and family.

> Then they can train the younger women to love their husbands and children, to be self-controlled and pure, to be *busy at home*, to be kind, and to be subject to their husbands, so that no one will malign the word of God. (Titus 2:5 NIV, emphasis added)

Being busy at home can be an honorable life. The work is never complete, as there are always more closets to clean, conversations to have, meals to prepare, and projects to do. We are busy bees when our work is diligent and when the fear of the Lord motivates our actions at home.

Honing In on "Busy"

We are invited to steward our homes as worship, yet we lose sight of that vision amidst the piles of laundry and stacked dishes.

Demands for our time and attention tempt us to respond with urgency (which is sometimes appropriate) instead of Spirit-led intentionality and peaceful laboring in our days.

To be busy simply means to be active. Our associations with busy are "hard-working, very little extra time, engaged, and motivated." I would suggest that there are two types of "busy at home": either haphazard or intentional. Look for your personal "busy style" in the chart below.

Haphazard Busy	Intentional Busy
No real plan for the day	Strong sense of the day's purpose and tasks
Flustered	Works peacefully
Responding to urgent needs	Can respond to the urgent, but keeps focused on the important
Works fast, head down and overwhelmed	Looks in the eyes of those in the home
Doesn't have a meal plan	Has a plan for meals, can be flexible
Struggles to say "no" to commitments	Can say "no" to unnecessary commitments
Quick to anger if interrupted	Serves cheerfully
Tends to be random with activity at home	Sets aside tasks to play with her children

Feels guilty for what she hasn't done yet	Asks for help when she needs it
Has lost sense of purpose or vision for family/home life	Is a vision-filled woman, humbled by what God has called her to, but joyfully aware of the responsibilities
Pressure and burden motivate her to move faster	Works peacefully, sometimes fast, but not stressed
Chaotic	Calm
Doesn't get to bed "on time"	Gets to bed "on time"
Shops with no plan	Keeps lists for shopping

Which kind of busy woman do you tend to be? A little of both? How can you move from being Haphazard Busy to Intentional Busy?

There are no easy formulas here. However, I believe the main ingredient in becoming intentional is the fear of the Lord. Our good God is with us throughout our days, and He pursues our hearts. He calls each of us to a particular life.

BUSY AND INTERRUPTED

Sometimes, we are so busy and focused on our agenda that we demand to finish our task even when we are interrupted. We get interrupted and distracted from what we are busily trying to accomplish. For me, interruptions are common temptations and reminders that my life is not my own. Interruptions expose the desires that are held too tightly.

My sinful responses to interruptions:

- I am not flexible.
- I don't answer with a gentle heart.
- I repay evil with evil.
- I don't bless those who persecute me, even if it is my kids.
- I resent any interruption.
- I feel angry when I don't get to do what I am trying to do.

If I am working, that is what I want to do. I want to focus wholeheartedly. I can worship more easily (I think) if I am immersed in whatever it is. My mind can focus, my heart engages, enjoys it, and I have fun.

When I am cooking, the last thing I want to do is stop twenty times to put a toy back together, put my daughter's hair in a ponytail, work through a sibling conflict, find a Star Wars character stuck behind the couch, talk with my oldest about selfishness, praise my younger son for his patience while I cook because he had just been complaining he would die of a hungry tummy, answer the phone, hold my daughter while I stir...

Find me in the kitchen at 5:00 p.m. and, if I haven't prepared dinner during nap time, this is my situation. The match of interruptions is lit and at any moment my sinful heart could ignite in frustration.

Yet, Interruptions Can Be Blessings, Not Burdens

How we interpret interruptions makes all the difference. If we value our agenda above God's, we hold our agenda tightly. With a clenched hand, we demand to stay on task. When we are interrupted, we can get angry at whatever or whoever got us off track. Resentful and raging, our hearts withhold love. The interruption is a burden, revealing our selfishness.

Or, if we see interruptions as blessings, we can respond with flexibility, empowered by the fear of the Lord. Jesus gives us these blessings to remind us whom we serve – Him – by serving those around us.

Furthermore, it is a miracle that God reminds me to be flexible, joyful, and obedient to His whisper in those interruptions. When I respond peacefully to my children, it is beautiful evidence of God's reign in my heart. Interruptions are God asking me to serve Him with flexibility, holding loosely my hopes for productivity and attention.

How do you respond to interruptions? What is going on in your heart?

WORSHIPFUL RESPONSES TO INTERRUPTIONS

Here are some ways I have experienced worshipful responses to interruptions in my pursuit of work.

- Respond graciously when the call, voice, or knock at door happens.

- My tone is gentle and attentive to whoever has a request.

- Though inconvenienced, I serve willingly, cheerfully.

- Letting go of hope of the completed task, I acknowledge my dependence on God.

- My thoughts shift from "my agenda" to whatever God has brought in front of me instead.

- My heart is humbled by requests that reveal my inability to accomplish anything apart from God's help.

- I see my work as opportunity to worship.

- I see Christ's loving pursuit of my heart as he gives me gifts (relationships with people and things) to steward.

In Titus, we are reminded to be "busy at home." God means for us to be worshipful about our busyness, so that most certainly means we are to fear Him and enjoy Him as we busily labor. Intentionality born from a heart that fears the Lord is duty with delight! We are dutifully serving Christ as we think about our days and how God wants us to spend them. His grace really does motivate.

REFLECTION QUESTIONS

1. When are you a busy-body?

2. What is the pay-off for knowing others' business?

3. What are you neglecting so that you can busy-body?

CHAPTER 20

From Sluggard to Steward

The earth is the LORD's, and everything in it, the world, and all who live in it.

(Ps. 24:1)

WHAT IS STEWARDSHIP?

"*Stewardship*: the conducting, supervising, or managing of something; *especially*: the careful and responsible management of something entrusted to one's care." [1]

Do you think that all that you have is really yours? Your home, family, friends… Are they *your* possessions? It is easy to believe this lie—that we own our stuff. But the truth is: all of it is from God. The idea that we are mere "managers" of God's stuff (because it is all His anyway) is laughable to most people. Our Western culture is heavy on materialism and on owning as much stuff as we can. We often ignore the fact that all these gifts are from God and instead believe, arrogantly, that we possess things and people.

> Every good gift and every perfect gift is from above, coming down from the Father of lights with whom there is no variation or shadow due to change. (James 1:17)

---

1   From the *Merriam Webster Dictionary*, http://www.merriam-webster.com/dictionary/stewardship, retrieved February 15, 2010.

We easily ignore the Giver. We often miss the big picture of how we are invited to interact with gifts on earth. God invites us to stewardship.

THE STEWARD CARES ABOUT WHAT THE MASTER CARES ABOUT

The earth is the LORD's and the fullness thereof. (Ps. 24:1a, KJV)

God gives us life, families, homes, and jobs to steward for His glory. We steward things, but we also steward God's grace through the responsibilities He has given: both the tangible and the intangible. To be a steward is to see everything in our lives as God's, not ours. As Master, He rules over every life, even though not all people acknowledge His supreme authority. Our responsibility to care for the earth reflects His care for us.

> For by him all things were created, in heaven and on earth, visible and invisible, whether thrones or dominions or rulers or authorities—all things were created through him and for him. And he is before all things, and in him all things hold together. (Col. 1:16-17)

The heart of a godly steward is humble—recognizing the joyful responsibility God has given to care for God's world and people. This humility, lived out, has meaning, depth, and purpose. A steward knows why she is stewarding and who she is working for. With conviction, working diligently, the steward fears God— knowing He is paying close attention to how she is caring.

Fear of the Lord humbles the steward daily with the knowledge of where her property/time/stuff comes from and whom it belongs to. As the steward stewards, she is mindful of God's presence and power over her.

A steward is faithful. She is humbled by the responsibility God entrusted to her and responds with faithfulness to God and to what she is stewarding.

Stewardship is an avenue by which we can express our gratitude to God when we recognize His provision.

For example: As a mother, I am stewarding young people. I get to feed, clothe, teach, discipline, and play with four people made in God's image—for Him! They are His children first. He has called me to steward them; He is always watching and helping me love them. He gives grace as I steward.

Characteristics of a Steward

A steward is:

- faithful

- diligent

- humble

- grateful

- persevering

- quick to give God credit

- grounded in the fear of the Lord

- thinking of others more highly than self

- focused on what God's purpose is in her

- confident she is loved by God

When I forget they are His children first, I have stepped into the world of the sinful sluggard. How I interact with God's gifts is by being either a steward or a sluggard.

A Bad Steward Is a Sluggard

> The soul of a sluggard craves and gets nothing, while the soul of the diligent is richly supplied. (Prov. 13:4)

If you don't have stewardship, you have the apathetic sluggard: she's forgotten who actually owns everything. The sluggard is inactive in body and/or in heart.

A sloth is an idle and lazy creature whose main goal for the day is to lie around. She moves only when necessary, and even then, very slowly. The sloth is the epitome of laziness. The sluggard's behavior reveals a deeper issue: a heart that does not fear God.

> Slothfulness casts into a deep sleep, and an idle person will suffer hunger. (Prov. 19:15)

> The sluggard buries his hand in the dish and will not even bring it back to his mouth. (Prov. 19:24)

The sin of the sluggard, deep down, is a sin of heart, not just lazy behavior. Do you identify with this struggle? Maybe outwardly you are busy, but your heart lacks desire, passion, and purpose. You don't look like a sluggard, but your heart is that of a sluggard's. Your life is harried, but visionless. You want to be a godly steward, but it seems far out of reach. So, you settle for what is familiar—half-heartedness.

> The sin of sloth can invade even the busiest life. In fact, it tends to infect lives that are too busy, full of too many things. Though we tend to lump sloth with laziness, it isn't necessarily physical idleness. It's more of an attitude, a spiritual idleness. The Latin term for it was *acedia*, which means "not caring." Slothful people might well run around doing everything or lie around doing nothing. The core problem, either way, is that they feel nothing. Down deep, they don't care. Sloth can be expressed both as do-nothingness—or extreme busyness that covers up the apathy within so that person doesn't have to face its core cause. —Ellen Vaughn[2]

There is good news. The sluggard can repent. God's grace is given to you so you can be forgiven and steward His grace. And He faithfully gives wisdom to you as you humbly ask for help. The very act of repentance is another gift from God you can steward!

As you see Jesus love you in your slothful, sluggardly ways, you can be redeemed from those beliefs and behaviors.

---

2   Vaughn, Ellen. *Time Peace* (Grand Rapids, MI: Zondervan, 2007), p. 88.

His grace is so massive you can't escape it. Furthermore, stewardship of His grace means you get an instantaneous opportunity to live out redemption. Your acknowledgement of your sin is a response of faith. God is lovingly reminding you that you are His precious child and that He hasn't rejected you because of your idle or restless heart. His grace is at work before you get to work. Just saying to God, "I am sorry I have been a sluggard. Please forgive me and give me courage to live as a steward" is an important action, stewarding His grace changing your heart.

Characteristics of a Sluggard:

- Aimless

- Idle

- Lazy

- Overwhelmed

- Ambivalent about others' approval of their home, life, work

- Too proud to ask for help

- Working hard on the wrong things

- Easily distracted

- Starts things, rarely finishes

- Not organized

- Impatient

- Apathetic

- Lacks ambition

- Shallow conviction

- May have a happy disposition, but deeply dissatisfied

- Restless heart under the appearance of rest.

STEWARDSHIP IN SEASON

> For everything there is a season, and a time for every matter under heaven. (Eccles. 3:1)

Everyone is in a different season of life. Maybe you are a college girl, an empty nester, or knee-deep in laundry piles and diapers. In each of our seasons, God invites us to worship. Furthermore, He gently calls us to stewardship.

With fear of the Lord motivating our meek demeanor, we respond to Jesus with worship. Our hearts depend on Christ and we are filled with joy to live lives that make Jesus look good. Our stewardship of both people and things looks different in each season.

WHAT SEASON ARE YOU IN?

As a young girl, I wanted to be an adult. When I was single, I wanted to be married. When my kids were babies, I wanted them to be preschoolers. As each season changed, my ambitious heart would often covet the next season. Even in my current season, I am tempted to grumble in it and look forward to a future time in the life of our family.

Each season I am given is an opportunity for worship. Yet, deep under the sporadic complaints and restless discontentment for my season lies a heart dissatisfied with what God has given me.

As God calls me to my season, He calls me to steward His grace in it. Each season is a calling—an invitation to worship with the day-to-day of life. When in college, my season was mostly about learning and growing spiritually. Stewardship in that season meant working hard in studies and learning from older women about being a woman.

When I worked outside the home, I was in relationship with many non-Christians. Stewardship of those relationships meant pursuing people with as much love and grace as I had opportunity to give. That season afforded more opportunities for evangelism, which I loved.

I am now in a season that involves staying home with four young children. Stewardship in my current season is about sacrificial service, which has brought me to my knees in overwhelming dependence on the Holy Spirit to keep my family and home running. More than checking things off a list, *I am called to steward the love and grace of God.* By stewarding my family and home, I get to display that grace. My children witness my redeemed heart needing Jesus every day.

Managing God's grace in my season calls me to humble service without grumbling. Being led moment by moment by God replaces merely going through the motions of my day. As God lovingly directs my work, I am more gracious and flexible with my duties. The gift and weight of this calling are intense and beautiful. And it is His grace that allows me to extend it to others. I am truly grateful I am in this season. I desire to steward it with repentance and continual and contagious worship.

What is your season? How can you more faithfully steward God's grace in it?

FROM SLUGGARD TO STEWARD
How does being a steward look?

- I will view my days as a gift of God's grace—then, in worship, steward them to His glory.

- I will work hard in humility, and my heart will be sensitive to the Holy Spirit to guide my steps.

- When I feel apathetic, I will remember how the gospel has changed my heart and life.

- Serving others is a joy, and a way of serving Jesus.

- Any good that comes from my work of godly stewardship is a gift of grace to God's glory, not my own.

- I am aware, in my heart, throughout my day, of evidences of God's grace.

- Giving my time, attention, and money to others increases my joy.

- When I get busy, I fight to remember why I am busy, increasing my worshipful knowledge of God's love, presence, and attention to my heart.

REFLECTION QUESTIONS

1. Where do you see godly stewardship in your life and heart?

2. Where do you see a sluggardly or slothful heart in your life?

3. What does redemption from being a sluggard look like for you?

4. Who do you know who might help you learn stewardship, practically?

CHAPTER 21

From Independence to Dependence

The essence of our work as humans must be that it is done in conscious reliance on God's power, and in conscious quest of God's pattern of excellence, and in deliberate aim to reflect God's glory.

John Piper[1]

"Do it by myself!" or "No, *I* do it." I heard those cantankerous words many times when my children were toddlers. Both adorable and aggravating, wiggling in independence, and not wanting the slightest help from me, they pushed my hands away as I tried to help them pull up their pants, tie a shoe, or wipe their noses. They resisted dependence and, instead, insisted they do it "by self." There is a natural independence that comes with a child growing older. I understand that, and I want that for our kids. But under the basic desire for independence, there's a whiff of that familiar, deeper rebellion my heart knows oh so well. It smells like my own life-long heart attitude toward God: "Do it by myself." Pushing God's loving help away, my soul insists on doing my life alone.

---

1   Piper, John. *Don't Waste Your Life* (Wheaton, IL: Crossway Publishers, 2003), p. 141.

Godless Independence = a Self-Sufficient Heart

Godless independence denounces, consciously or unconsciously, the presence of God in our lives. It says to God, "I've got this one, thank you very much. I can do it without you."

But that is not the way we are supposed to live.

> Such is the confidence that we have through Christ toward God. Not that we are sufficient in ourselves to claim anything as coming from us, but our sufficiency is from God, who made us sufficient to be ministers of a new covenant, not of the letter but of the Spirit. For the letter kills, but the Spirit gives life. (2 Cor. 3:4-6)

We are born resisting God's help. That urge to *go it alone* is a battle within our own heart. It is in opposition to God's loving, enabling grace for us. We don't want His intimate help. We would rather fight Him and try to prove that we can do it by ourselves.

Made in God's image, we belong to Him and are made for His glory. Since the Fall, God's beloved kids have foolishly claimed, "I know best." From our career aspirations to choosing a spouse...*we know best?* What? That can't be right. How about the little things: our schedules, our friendships, our tasks. Did we forget God is paying attention to the details of our lives? Do we really believe we can chart our own course? Yet we often choose to forget His care for us.

This sin is as old as Adam and Eve and touches every person's heart. Mine included.

A few years ago, I had a convicting image come to mind when describing this godless independence. The picture was of me walking along, focused, driven, and Jesus was holding my hand, graciously enabling each event, relationship, and task in my life. In my independence, I shook His hand from my own, asserting that I didn't need His help, but still wanted Him near. Before I knew it, my ambitious, independent heart denied any help from God and pretty much ignored His presence.

My independent heart declares I have a better idea and agenda for my life and actions throughout my day. My sinful desires want to accomplish life and deny the supernatural enabling grace of the Holy Spirit. This godless independence embraces the lie, "I can make it on my own."

Thankfully, that isn't the whole picture. As much fit-throwing as I do, God has promised to be my Father. He made a promise to me, and my immature and independent heart can't drive Him away. *He doesn't let me shake His hand away! He never leaves. His love is persistent.*

His help is perfect. And He is constantly, lovingly, helping us.

> I lift up my eyes to the hills. From where does my help come? My help comes from the LORD, who made heaven and earth. He will not let your foot be moved; he who keeps you will not slumber. Behold, he who keeps Israel will neither slumber nor sleep. The LORD is your keeper; the LORD is your shade on your right hand. The sun shall not strike you by day, nor the moon by night. The LORD will keep you from all evil; he will keep your life. The LORD will keep your going out and your coming in from this time forth and forevermore. (Ps. 121)

INDEPENDENCE FROM GOD IS A MIRAGE

We can't actually shake God's help away. He loves His children too much. He resists our resistance. And He wins the fight. His pursuit and presence defeats our foolish independence.

There is nothing we can do without His grace. His grace is so present in everything we do, though we can't see it. It is like air: we desperately need it, but deny its power in our lives. God's grace breathes life into every action, decision, hour of sleep. From our salvation to daily life, grace is the constant oxygen.

To think we could do anything apart from God's help and grace reveals pride and self-sufficiency. This sin, when carried out to its fullest, is the horrific belief that we could actually pay the price for our sin. Godless independence says, "I will die for myself."

It is His grace at work right now through the Holy Spirit convicting you of independence from Him and deepening your love for Jesus. God is still holding your hand.

JESUS WAS DEPENDENT ON HIS FATHER

Periodically, I think of my Lord Jesus as a baby. I marvel at the Incarnation. Trying to wrap my brain around that point of theology is overwhelming. Nonetheless, I imagine Jesus sometimes as a young boy because I have two sons. Sometimes we talk about Jesus as a son and how He never sinned, always obeying His Father.

Jesus shows me how to depend on God. He matured physically, yet He still depended on His Father. Even as a grown man, He still needed His Father. It is worshipful for me to offer my weakness, boast in it, and, with empty hands, depend on God, as worship.

> Jesus was the first person who didn't seek independence. He wanted to be in continuous contact with his heavenly Father.—Paul Miller[2]

When tempted in the wilderness, Jesus appealed to the Father and quoted Scripture to fight against Satan. Jesus, again, is our perfect model for what dependence looks like. Jesus as God shows me that, while He was incarnate, He depended on His Father.

THE DISCOMFORT OF DEPENDENCE

> A truly humble man is sensible of his natural distance from God; of his dependence on Him; of the insufficiency of his own power and wisdom; and that it is by God's power that he is upheld and provided for, and that he needs God's wisdom to lead and guide him, and His might to enable him to do what he ought to do for Him.—Jonathan Edwards[3]

Dependence and humility are not my natural inclinations. I resist asking for help when I really need it. Sometimes, in the face of overwhelming duty and burden—lip bit and heart

---

2   Miller, Paul. *The Praying Life* (Colorado Springs, CO: NavPress, 2009), p. 70.

3   Edwards, Jonathan. *Christian Love As Manifested in Heart and Life* (New York: Robert Carter & Brothers, 1954), p. 193.

racing—I avoid the opportunity for others to help me and, with a determined mind, try to get it done (on my own).

To depend on God or others, we must first be aware of our need. If I am overwhelmed and stressed to the max and am not aware of my weakness and need, I am blind. Blinded by my independence, I foolishly think I can accomplish my work alone. Admitting our weakness requires honest self-assessment and lots of practice if you are prone to godless independence like me. God's grace enables us to see our need, and it's His grace that enables our humility to depend on Him and others to meet our needs.

DEPENDENCE AS WORSHIP
How do we depend on God, worshipfully?

- Admit weakness.

- Talk to your Father God about the challenge you are facing.

- Ask for help; don't demand it.

- When helped by God and others, see it as a gift of grace.

- Look deeply for the ways God loves you in the details of the challenge.

- Thank Him for His attention and presence.

- Thank Him for the gift of weakness and dependence, because His power and strength are made perfect in it.

REFLECTION QUESTIONS

1. Have you ever seen godless independence in your heart?

2. What does it look like to accept help from God and others?

3. Where are you most resistant to accepting help?

4. How might you embrace your weakness today?

CHAPTER 22

From Grumbling to Gratitude

DO YOU GRUMBLE?

Have you ever complained, protested, or murmured? Assuming all of us have, let's explore and uncover what grumbling is and why we do it. Then, we will see how God invites us to express gratitude instead of grumbling.

Paul Tripp says, "Grumbling is the background drone of a discontented heart."[1] In other words, whatever my circumstance, when I don't think it is good or right for me, I whine, kick, and complain to God: *This is not good.*

Where does grumbling come from? We desire a certain reality, and when it doesn't happen, we are tempted to grumble, and sometimes, we give in.

YOU CAN'T GRUMBLE IF YOU DON'T DESIRE

Desires are from God. Made in His image to reflect His grace and glory, we are designed to desire. Our hopes and dreams are meant to reflect God's grace and love.

For example: If I desire my house to be organized and clean, that is a good desire, stemming from a heart that wants orderliness, cleanliness, and godly stewardship—an act of worship to make Jesus look good. If my desire is held in my hand

---

1   Paul David Tripp, "Grumbling—A Look at a 'Little' Sin," *Journal of Biblical Counseling* 18 (Winter 2000): 51.

loosely, I can be flexible when my family's needs keep me from cleaning. If I want the house to be clean above anything else, that loosely held desire, instead, gets squeezed, and my clenched-fist desire makes a demand for a clean house. And I grumble because I don't get what I want.

James 1:14 says, "Each person is tempted when he is lured and enticed by his own evil desire." Our desires are already present in our hearts before the temptation presents itself. Because of sin, our good desires turn dark. Desires are to be held loosely, with fear and trembling before the Lord, knowing He is paying loving and close attention to us. We can trust Him to work things out for us, His children.

> Then desire when it has conceived gives birth to sin, and sin when it is fully grown brings forth death. (James 1:15)

Desires often lead to disappointment. When we don't get what we want, it is an opportunity to resist temptation. We can acknowledge the disappointment with God. He is with us, comforting us in the sadness of disappointment. He isn't surprised. He is very much aware of what is happening. If it hurts, He is also there with us to comfort our hearts.

DESIRES AND DISAPPOINTMENTS AREN'T SINFUL

In that moment when our hearts squeeze that desire tighter, we've become discontent and full of grumbling because we did not receive. Discontentment and grumbling are best friends. They speak the same angry language. They yell: *God doesn't have a good plan for me after all!* We may throw a bitter, silent fit in our heart, or flat out scream. Both represent a heart that is angry—ultimately at God.

We *desire*; we get *disappointed*; we feel *discontent*; then we *demand*.[2]

---

2   Tripp, Paul David. *Instruments in the Redeemers' Hands* (Phillipsburg, NJ: P&R Publishing, 2002), pp. 85-8.

Another way to understand desires is to see desires as unfulfilled blessings. We desire good, and to enjoy any kind of good is to receive a blessing, a gift from God. He gives good gifts to His kids. Sometimes, we receive His gifts gratefully: a promotion, a redeemed relationship, beauty, wealth, a baby, opportunities, a favor—the list goes on.

When others are blessed by God, *sometimes* we're grateful for them too. But at other times, we demand and envy. The three-headed monster of sinful desires is: bitterness, jealousy, and envy. In Scripture, this monster of sin causes discontentment and rivalry, which destroy relationships. It starts with comparing what they have to what you lack. Temptation whispers, "Why do they have that and I don't?" and the envious heart responds, "Why not *me*, Lord?"

Envy Compares
Sadly, I have heard these confessions from countless women: "Comparisons are really depressing me lately," or "Why can't my husband be like hers?" or "I'm unhappy because my life doesn't look like hers." My own envy has sounded like, "Why can't my post-pregnancy body bounce back like hers?"

Envy Kills
Everyone in our lives possesses something we don't. We often secretly resent others' blessings. I have envied friends' weight losses, vacations, or nearby family members. My envy has threatened those relationships. When we stew on what we don't have, we waste away, for "envy rots the bones" (Prov. 14:30).

Envy Is Evil
Envy is selfish and resentful and is often joined by jealousy and coveting. "But if you have bitter jealousy and selfish ambition in your hearts, do not boast and be false to the truth" (James 3:14).

Envy is another side of demanding. We demand what we haven't gotten yet, revealing sin. And sin is treason against God, which brings death.

We don't want to be separated from God, and Christ has made a perfect way to be reconciled to the Father. Through

His death on the cross, we have forgiveness of our sin. With soft hearts, we can bring our grumbling, envious hearts to Jesus and be cleansed. This grace is thorough, continuous, and we are completely made new. So wonderful!

REPLACING ENVY WITH ENJOYMENT OF GOD

Thank God we can repent of sinful desires, grumbling, envy, and ingratitude. Jesus meets us with open arms, forgiving us and lavishing grace on us. Because of Christ's death in our place, we can stand loved, covered in righteousness. Grace changes us and the Holy Spirit gives us worship-filled desires!

Fighting grumbling is ongoing, yet pretty simple. We must remember who God is and who we are. We exchange grumbling for gratitude if we have a firm belief in who God is. As we see God as a Holy King, yet personal and loving us like a faithful daddy, we can take a sigh of relief, knowing He is working out the details. Grumbling is the opposite of this restful knowledge, nervously doubting God's goodness. If, in the face of disappointment, we remember our loving daddy is still present with us, gratitude flows from our hearts. We see His faithfulness instead of allowing disappointment to arouse grumbling.

REPLACING GRUMBLING WITH GRATITUDE

Gratitude is about sweet awareness of God's Fatherly concern over our lives. When we interpret the details of our lives with firm belief that He loves us, we are more likely to be grateful instead of grumbling. We will not grow in gratitude if we resist the truth that God is a Father who delights in His children.

At the intersection of disappointment, we can either believe God's way is good or demand that our way is better.

For example: My day is not going like I planned. I have already had to switch around the schedule twice. I didn't sit down to write as soon as I had hoped. My desire to study has been thwarted. I feel disappointed. I am tempted to grumble. As the Holy Spirit prompts my heart, I am slightly aware of this soul temptation. If I am angry enough, I just might throw a fit (my unfulfilled desires might give birth to sin). But, there is another way for my heart: I can realize the disappointment and still know who God is. I must combat my disappointment with belief. Has God abandoned me? No. He loves me and is present with me. I am not defined by my unfulfilled desires. Instead of grumbling and demanding, I must remember who my God is. This is worship, sisters! As Jesus fills me with gratitude, I remember that these good desires are to be held loosely, because my biggest desire of all is to enjoy Jesus. Redeemed desires!

REDEEMED DESIRES

A joyful heart that enjoys God and grows in gratitude is one that resists the sin of grumbling with its foundation of unbelief. Believing and remembering God's steadfast love brings gratitude, and He delights in us! We get to rest in God's steadfast love.

> But the LORD takes pleasure in those who fear him, in those who hope in his steadfast love. (Ps. 147:11)

We can, because of God's abundant grace, resist grumbling and instead worship Jesus with gratitude. We grumble when we forget God's goodness and nearness to us. So, let's cultivate gratitude for Jesus' constant love for us, and worship.

> Remembering our dependence on past mercies kindles gratitude. Gratitude is past-oriented dependence; faith is future-oriented dependence. Both forms of dependence are humble, self-forgetting and God-exalting. If we do not believe that we are deeply dependent on God for all we have or hope to have, then the very spring of gratitude and faith runs dry.
> —John Piper[3]

---

3   Piper, John. *A Godward Life* (Sisters, OR: Multnomah Publishers, 1997), p. 46.

REFLECTION QUESTIONS

1. Are you aware of how desires shape your days?

2. How do you respond to daily disappointments?

3. Who do you envy?

4. When does gratitude flow from your heart freely?

5. How does remembering the love of Jesus help replace your heart's grumbling with gratitude?

6. When you think of God's fatherly delight in you, are you more likely to accept disappointment graciously?

CHAPTER 23

From Isolation to Community

When relationships are built around the truths of the gospel—the truth that we are walking in light even though we are still sinners in need of cleansing by his blood—we can be free from feelings of inferiority and the demanding spirit that is born of pride. We can pursue relationships without fear of being discovered as the sinners we are. This kind of open relationship rests solely on the realities of the gospel. We are more sinful and flawed than we ever dared believe, and so is everyone we know. Because of this, we won't be surprised by others' sins. They won't expect us to be sinless either, so we don't have to give in to self-condemnation and fear when they see us as we really are. We don't have to hide or pretend anymore.

Elyse Fitzpatrick[1]

---

1   Fitzpatrick, Elyse M. and Johnson, Dennis E. *Counsel From the Cross* (Wheaton, IL: Crossway, 2009), p. 86.

CREATED FOR COMMUNITY

We were created for community. The Father, Son, and Spirit are one, living in constant, holy communion. Theologians have been writing about this magnificent community for centuries, and yet, there is still mystery. We can't fathom what that community looks like; it is out of our scope of understanding. We yearn to know something of this perfect intimacy. In Christ, we do have intimacy with God: miraculous, beautiful, awe-inspiring, and tender. However, because of our sinful nature, this intimacy is tainted. We long to be united in perfect community with God someday.

Walking with Jesus and being redeemed by Him bring a deep-down peace, knowing He knows us and still accepts us. We are in community with God. When we are burdened or blessed, we talk things through with Him first. We hide in Him as refuge when we are afraid. Our community experience with people is shaped by our community experience with Jesus.

Would you say that you enjoy community with God? Are you close to Him? Do you run to Him daily? For comfort, care, relationship?

If our relationship to God is vertical, our relationship to others is horizontal. We may experience wonderful, consistent relationship to God, yet our horizontal connections can be random and rarely helpful in our lives.

The following portrays some characteristics of common community experiences with God and others. See if you see yourself or a loved one described.

Are you connected to God but not to people?

You may have rich moments studying your Bible that leave you fulfilled and encouraged, yet your heart feels a little lonely, because you aren't in relationship with sisters or brothers with whom you share your thoughts. Your faith is stirred but doesn't get worked out in close relationships with others.

Maybe you've taken a risk, confessed sin or a struggle, and have been shamed by a lack of love in response. Courage was met with little grace, resulting in disappointment. You try to seek meaningful friendships, and no one seems to get it. You feel isolated and are ambivalent about trying again. You definitely want deep relationship that is purposeful and focused on pursuing each other. You want the "iron sharpens iron" kind of relationships. Hoping for this feels too vulnerable. Maybe you settle for isolation, wondering if you will ever have real community. Isolation feels like the better option. Risking your heart for the sake of intimacy again is too scary.

Or you may be angry, bitter because you expect people to love you well and they don't. So instead of being patient and proactive in community, you sit back and judge. You'd rather glare in disappointment than gracefully hope. So, you are connected and growing in Christ, while nursing your wounds of disappointment. You blindly aim your bitterness, judging others.

Are you connected to God and overly connected to people?

Occasionally our journey of faith is intended by God to be walked alone, because we have become too dependent on others. God sometimes empties us of overly dependent relationships so we are made aware of our idolatry of people, an unhealthy need for intimacy.

This can be a subtle experience or a dramatic one. It might be a sign that you are overly dependent on others if you go to a friend when you are hurting before you go to God. You may find life in both, but you get more out of your talk with your friend. If you have friends who are good listeners, then talking through your struggle with one may be a quick fix. However, if the help you get from others doesn't push you back to Jesus for counsel, comfort, and restoration, then your friends are not loving you best.

Are you numb to God and people?

Perhaps you have been a Christian so long you don't remember *not* walking with Jesus. But maybe you have forgotten the zeal you once knew. Have you become cold to Christ? Are you so used to the traditions that come with the Christian life that you need to wake up to the radical grace that is yours, in Christ?

When was the last time you confessed a dark struggle in your heart with a friend and tasted the sweetness of God's acceptance? Are you more committed to church, your acts of service, and socializing at church, than being uncomfortable and exposed for your lack of repentance in your life? Are you hiding in your Christianity? Has your Christian journey become a chore, a part of life, yet you aren't learning anything new about Jesus? When you read your Bible, are you thinking, *Yes, I know this*, or *God, I am amazed you are always teaching me new things about who you are*?

Maybe you are so disillusioned that you have forgotten what passion for Jesus and tender, humble connection with believers look like. You've lost the awe. Being disappointed by God and the sinners in your life has left you cynical. You'd rather just go to church and be "good" than expect more from community. You've become numb to God and His people. Being a church-goer has become your identity, not being loved by Jesus.

My intent is not to condemn, but to perhaps name your struggle with community. I want to remind and invite you to worshipful Christian community. No matter where you find yourself in relationship to God or His people, we all can grow in living this out, which is worship. God invites us into true community with Him first, via His Spirit. We embrace the Holy Spirit and worship in community.

WHAT IS CHRISTIAN COMMUNITY?

> So, being affectionately desirous of you, we were ready to share with you not only the gospel of God but also our own selves, because you had become very dear to us. (1 Thess. 2:8)

God gives us friends so that we can encourage one another. As we share, we are demonstrating selfless, sacrificial care that comes from a good God. Connected to people by grace for our encouragement and redemption, we are changed over time. This can be as practical as meeting needs or as emotional as helping a friend process pain.

Furthermore, we are brothers and sisters in Christ, joyfully pursuing one another with the love of Jesus. Like family, we know that through trials and triumphs we stand together.

Created for community, when we live this out, we are imaging God. When the gospel is the central theme of community, our gaze is on Him, fighting for faith for one another. It is a demonstration of redemption, as we aren't afraid to get our hands dirty with the dealings of sin. God gives us courage to share our struggles and confess sin in community. We are shown God's forgiveness as we are forgiven by others. We are walking honestly, provoking and inspiring one another—embracing who we are and those whom we love.

CHARACTERISTICS OF CHRISTIAN COMMUNITY
Some of the key attributes of Christian fellowship are:

- Personal repentance and holiness as we are renewed in the image of Christ (Rom. 5–8; 2 Cor. 3:18; Eph. 4:21-24).

- Joyful satisfaction in Christ (Phil. 3:1-11).

- Authenticity fueled by grace and humility, and committed to reconciliation (Eph. 4:1-3; Col. 3:12-17).

- Sacrificial love, encouragement, and service for one another (John 15:12-13; 17:20-23; Eph. 5:1-2; Heb. 10:25; 1 Pet. 4:10; 1 John 1:1-10).

- Dependence on prayer and the Holy Spirit's power (Rom. 8; Phil. 4:6-7).

- Unwavering faith in the promises of God (Rom. 4:20-21).

WE ARE EXPOSED AND LOVED
Honest, ongoing relationships are characterized by being exposed in our sin and reminding one another of our desperate need for God's grace daily. We are invited to remind one another of how loved we truly are, even as we sin. This is good news!

> The gospel of justifying faith means that while Christians are, in themselves still sinful and sinning, yet in Christ, in God's sight, they are accepted and righteous. So we can say that we are more wicked than we ever dared believe, but more loved and accepted in Christ than we ever dared hope—at the very same time. This creates a radical new dynamic for personal growth. It means that the more you see your own flaws and sins, the more precious, electrifying, and amazing God's grace appears to you. But on the other hand, the more aware you are of God's grace and acceptance in Christ, the more able you are to drop your denials and self-defenses and admit the true dimensions and character of your sin.—Timothy Keller[2]

We are sisters, journeying honestly, wrestling sin, and growing in our worship. We can drop our self-protection and risk those parts of our hearts that have been isolated and held in secrecy.

Personally, I have a few close female friends who fight for me. If I am hurting or struggling to believe God is with me, I know that as I share, my friends will accept me and remind me of God's affection, attention, and approval. They fight for me, helping me remember God's steadfast love. What a gift from God to give me friends that help me see the gospel at work in my heart. I feel blessed by friends who care for me.

We Have to Fight for Friendship

No one has "extra" time to spend deeply connecting in community. To invest in relationships that give life, pointing us to the cross of Jesus, takes time. It is selfless, sacrificial service to grow a friendship. It can take a long time, but if Jesus is the point of the relationship, it will be an investment that always pays off. Friendship is worth the fight!

---

2   Keller, Tim. *Paul's Letter to the Galatians: Living in Line with the Truth of the Gospel*, Redeemer Presbyterian Church, 2003, 2. Quoted in "More than we ever dared hope," http://firstimportance.org/more-than-we-ever-dared-hope, retrieved December 9, 2012.

Why fight? Because we forget. Friends help us fight when we forget.

- We forget who we are. We need to be reminded who we are.

- We forget why we work. We need to be reminded why we work.

- We forget who we worship. We need to be reminded who we worship.

- We forget we are loved. We need to be reminded of Jesus' great love for us.

- We forget the fear of the Lord. We need to be fought for to remember the fear of the Lord.

While Christ is the most faithful friend we can ever have, He does bless us with sisters who love Him and love us well. They fight for our hearts when we forget. They are the "iron that sharpens iron." A friend living out community with us is a safe place for us to confess sin and to bear burdens. This interdependence is a gift from the Lord that we can humbly ask for and receive.

REFLECTION QUESTIONS

1. Have you had a distorted experience with Christian community?

2. What characteristic of Christian community resonates most with you?

3. Who are the people in your life who fight for your heart and are your "iron sharpening iron"? For whose heart do you fight?

4. Who do you hide from? Is there something about your life and/or heart that you want to keep a secret?

PART FIVE:

A Woman's Home

CHAPTER 24

A Beautiful Heart, A Beautiful Home

Like a gold ring in a pig's snout is a beautiful woman without discretion.

(Prov. 11:22)

WE LOVE BEAUTY

Learning how to become a beautiful woman and have a beautiful home is not the aim of this chapter; exploring the relationship between beauty and peace from God is. As with the other ideas in this book, it's nothing new, but is an invitation to respond to God with worship.

We live in an age where we are bombarded by visual beauty, often completely unrealistic and lacking discretion. Airbrushed, provocative, and wrinkle-free, our world's image of feminine beauty is far from honest or modest. We are tempted to fixate on outward beauty, and it is a false and fleeting sight. The carrot of perfection is always beyond our reach as our tempted hearts continue to inch forward, hoping to attain it.

Beauty is from God because He himself is beautiful. Made in His image, we all long for beauty, whether we realize it or not. A sunset, a newborn baby, or a close look at a flower: we gaze in admiration as our souls catch a glimpse of God's glory.

Something so beautiful we can hardly believe it is real stirs an appetite for God. He is the author of such majesty.

Recently, I was standing with my family at the top of a mountain in the Pacific Northwest, looking down over twelve small islands. We could see the sea for a hundred miles, all the way to Canada. I found myself hardly breathing. I was frozen, captivated by creation. Remembering to take breaths, my eyes filled with tears. How could something so beautiful be witnessed and not accompany belief in a glorious Creator? God made beauty, and we are invited to enjoy it.

As we engage in our culture, we often notice excellence, creativity, and beauty all around. We see beauty in visual arts, architectural marvels, and even in our neighbor's living rooms. A room decorated with artistic skill and imagination draws us in, inspiring creativity. Visual beauty communicates intentional creativity—an example of God's handiwork.

BEAUTY'S COMPLEXITY

We strive to attain and express beauty, but often miss why it's such a challenge. We want beautiful bodies and homes, but we forget to look at the inside. Outward beauty may inspire worship to God, yet if our hearts are not being changed by Jesus, outward beauty is as fake as an airbrushed face in a cosmetic ad.

> Charm is deceptive, and beauty is fleeting; but a woman who fears the LORD is to be praised. (Prov. 31:30, NIV)

We purchase endless beauty products and spend large amounts of time looking at interior design ideas, but neglect to clothe our hearts in the fear of the Lord. Fearing the Lord dresses us, revealing Christ's love. Our appearance is radiant because of the work of Christ transforming us. His love is the truest form of beauty.

Physically, we are slowly dying, as is the world around us, both subject to the curse of sin (Rom. 8:21). Decay and death eventually replace our health and vibrancy. As the seasons take their toll, we see beauty take different turns.

Spiritually, we are renewed each day as our hearts fear the Lord. Worshiping Jesus makes us more radiant than any physical (and fading) alteration. There is no lasting hope in our outer selves; the unseen is more beautiful. Eventually, we start to notice beauty differently. We see past wrinkles and messes; we see hearts that fear the Lord. The peace of Christ shines brightly, radiating beauty.

BEAUTIFUL HEARTS, BEAUTIFUL HOMES

> For we are the aroma of Christ to God among those who are being saved and among those who are perishing. (2 Cor. 2:15)

We are the aroma, pronouncing Jesus' victory over our lives. We have the opportunity to be the aroma of Christ in all aspects of life. We represent His beauty. Homes, like our bodies, can be outwardly beautiful but inwardly chaotic and sinful. Our homes may be beautifully decorated, or clean and orderly, but beneath the surface, in the hearts of the people, is ugliness. Gorgeous and artful homes do not necessarily represent the hearts of their inhabitants. A house may be a glorious mansion, but its owner, a murderer. You can have an orderly home and a messy heart. Appearance is often a misrepresentation. Does the beauty we present outwardly honestly represent what is in our hearts? What is the aroma (unseen) and appearance (seen) of your home?

And, the flip side is true too. A messy house doesn't necessarily mean the hearts of its people are messy. Sometimes, the most beautiful homes are the ones with happy giggles from young children that are known for creating messes in every room. A happy, messy home may be chaotic outwardly, but the aroma of that home is loving and peaceful.

EXAMPLES OF HOMES AND HEARTS

Have you ever been in a home that was like a cold museum? You were afraid to touch anything. My guess is that the owners were not laid-back, casual, kick-your-feet-up, vulnerable people. If the house could talk, it would say: *My people are uptight, nervous, vain, and controlling.* The aroma of these homes doesn't communicate the peace of Christ. I am not comfortable in these homes, because I can smell the chaotic stench of their hearts. It seems like museum homes portray perfection, a misrepresentation of the heart. Many women have told me stories of how their parents worked constantly on the inside and outside of the home, making everything perfect—to impress others or keep a self-imposed standard. These women longed for attention from their parents and often develop a resistance to orderliness or perfectly cleaned homes because of the price they paid for it growing up.

I'm not saying an exceptionally clean and perfectly decorated home is bad. We do want to express beauty creatively in our homes, stewarding God's creativity with excellence. And some people really do have time and ability to keep a beautiful home. The emphasis here is on the heart and how beauty flows from it, not into it from beautiful surroundings.

To reiterate: beauty apart from the peace of Christ is fleeting and vain. To know Christ brings peace that results in inward *and* outward beauty. Often, though, with the "perfect" homes, you will discover owners that are gripped by fear of man, overly concerned with the opinions of others. So, beauty is sought—and spoiled—through control and vanity.

If you are someone who struggles with this, know that Christ is beautiful for you. God is not impressed with your appearance (home or body). He delights in you because of Jesus. Because Jesus is perfect beauty, you can breathe in the truth that you can be vulnerable, weak, and exposed for your desires to impress. His delight is constant, even as you strive for perfection. Grace is yours, a free gift, based on nothing you have done.

In contrast, have you ever been in a really messy house? My guess is that its owner is not bending over backwards apologizing for the many messes. The people who live there are used to it and welcome you into the chaos. Many of these homes have busy families or stewards that are either unable or ill-equipped to manage their homes. My experience in these homes is that the owner is honest. They know their home isn't perfect. They may feel shame over it, but the non-verbal communication is: *What you see is what you get. I am a mess, and I know it.* I feel more comfortable in these homes, because they feel honest. I can share the mess of my heart more naturally here.

If you are someone who is the "laid-back, honest, messy type," it is possible that you have wrongly excused the mess in the name of your "season." Neither perfect order nor messes should define our homes; the peace of Christ should. Sometimes messy homes are the result of an unrepentant sluggard who excuses herself from trying to learn organization, stewardship, and admitting her inability to grow in this area. As we've already seen, sluggardliness is a heart issue.

God invites us to stewardship, in the tension between the honesty of the ongoing mess and the hard work required to maintain order. He wants us to work hard to steward what He has given us but not to put our hope in it. We can too easily live for the approval of others and our self-view, which is vanity. If we steward our homes, knowing the peace of Christ, we don't hope in our physical appearance, whether bodies or homes. The peace of Christ becomes the greatest experience in the home, more than the mess or the order, as we know Him more.

TRUE BEAUTY

Knowing Jesus brings true peace to our hearts, which is the most prominent feature of our homes and bodies. As we serve our families and friends in our homes, what do they experience? Are they nervous to set a glass on your table? Or, on the other extreme, do they feel free to open up your cabinet and get their own water? Your heart's peace sets the tone for your home. That peace comes from knowing the power of God to change your heart.

True beauty is Christ in us. No amount of beauty or cleaning products ultimately improve our home's or our body's appearance. We can embrace Jesus more as we let loose our grip on vanity— hoping in Him instead of our appearance.

> Do not let your adorning be external—the braiding of hair and the putting on of gold jewelry, or the clothing you wear—but let your adorning be the hidden person of the heart with the imperishable beauty of a gentle and quiet spirit, which in God's sight is very precious. (1 Pet. 3:3-4)

OUR REDEEMED BEAUTY

Knowing that God himself is Beauty, we can embrace ways to express it creatively. We take into account our season and steward our homes, bodies, and work accordingly. We worship in our stewardship of both our homes and bodies when our gaze is on Jesus. Working on our bodies and homes can be an act of worship because we know that God gave us both to make Him look good.

The outward is the overflow of the inward belief in what is most beautiful. Jesus fills us up with His beauty, making us beautiful in heart and appearance. Our homes are more peaceful and sometimes more orderly. Our hearts are more peaceful and often more beautiful—because of Jesus.

REFLECTION QUESTIONS

1. Is your home one in which guests feel comfortable?

2. Do you have a standard of beauty for yourself? For your home?

3. How do you view yourself when your home is less than clean? What does this response reveal about your heart?

4. Do you see working on your heart as being as important as working on your home?

5. What would repentance look like in your relationship to beauty?

6. How might you grow in humility with your body and your home?

7. What do you want the aroma of your home to be?

CHAPTER 25

Practicing Biblical Hospitality

You shall treat the stranger who sojourns with you as the native among you, and you shall love him as yourself, for you were strangers in the land of Egypt: I am the LORD your God.

(Lev. 19:34)

We can hardly talk about work as worship and not talk about hospitality. I don't mean an outward understanding of hospitality: freshly folded towels and breakfast buffets at hotels or a fancy dinner that you've prepared in your home for your closest friends. No, true hospitality is sacrificial, uncomfortable, and does not seek to impress others. Hospitality flows from a hospitable heart. It is more about your open heart and home, not your impressive entertaining skills.

It is only in the last few hundred years that the understanding of hospitality changed. Western culture has reduced true hospitality to little more than providing food. Historically, humble and honest hospitality was experienced as part of culture. Meeting the needs of others was part of the function of a village, community life. Helping others survive and thrive was an act of service because the core of hospitality is to count others more significant than ourselves. Sure, there were still selfish motives in the mix, but something about cultural hospitality has shifted.

> Do nothing from selfish ambition or conceit, but in humility
> count others more significant than yourselves. (Phil. 2:3)

Tragically, over time, our selfishness has blended with individual-
ism and cultural segregation, making us distant from one another,
tending to hide our need for hospitality. We don't experience
life together anymore. It used to be commonplace to knock on
a stranger's door and be hosted for the night. Denying our needs
and pulling ourselves up by our bootstraps have resulted in a deep
lack of humble hospitality.

WHAT IS BIBLICAL HOSPITALITY?

In the Bible, the original Greek word for hospitality is *philoxenia*,
which means *love of strangers* (cf. Rom. 12:13). Hospitality is also:

- A means of honoring and loving Christ by meeting the needs
  of the poor (Prov. 14:31).

- To be practiced without grumbling, complaining or thought
  of reward (1 Pet. 4:9).

- Literally, "a love for strangers" (Heb. 13:1-2), treating
  fellow believers (Rom. 12:3; 1 Tim. 3:2), widows, orphans
  (1 Tim. 5:1-16), unbelievers (Luke 5:29), the poor and needy
  (Luke 14:12-14), missionaries (Matt. 10:9-11; Luke 10:5-16),
  foreigners, immigrants, refugees (Gen. 18:1-22), and even
  enemies (Rom. 12:20) as if they were your very own family.

- Helping the poor with no expectation of repayment
  (Prov. 19:17).

- Meeting the basic needs of others. This can include preparing
  food, providing lodging, giving physical protection, sharing
  material possessions, offering a place of rest, encouraging
  and sharing the love of Jesus.

Biblical hospitality is when we give ourselves willingly to
the needs of others. It is bigger than food and shelter. It is the
outpouring of mercy and grace from God to others, without

expectation for reciprocation. Jesus said in Luke 14:12b-13, "When you give a dinner or a banquet, do not invite your friends or your brothers or your relatives or rich neighbors, lest they also invite you in return and you be repaid. But when you give a feast, invite the poor, the crippled, the lame, the blind, and you will be blessed, because they cannot repay you. For you will be repaid at the resurrection of the just."

WHO ARE WE TO BE HOSPITABLE TOWARD?

Friends, family, church-members, co-workers, and strangers. How do you feel about inviting a stranger over to your home? We need to be hospitable to our own families first, as that is our first priority for giving our attention and service. Yet, we miss a grand opportunity for worship if we are only serving those who are already entrusted to our care.

Welcoming Neighbors

Our neighbors are those within our community who live life near us. Hospitality begins at home with our own families, then our neighbors. If we know those near us, we are likely aware of their needs. We can extend hospitality by providing love through food, sharing resources and friendship.

Welcoming Strangers

When we hear the word *stranger,* we may feel shy or uncomfortable. Yet, we are invited to love strangers. We may give our service and resources to strangers out of a sense of duty only, all the while staying distant. *Strangers might get us dirty*, we think. Needy or not, we can't control their expectations of us. Opening our hearts, lives, and homes to strangers requires that we die to our individualistic ideals. We must see strangers as significant, better than ourselves. We need wisdom and discernment as we invite strangers into our lives. We don't want to put ourselves or any of our family members in danger for the sake of hospitality. While God is worshiped in our love for others—including the love of strangers—it is not His will to risk harm to ourselves or our

family, if there are warning signs. Pray for wisdom. Check your
desire and decision with a trusted friend before you act.

> Do not neglect to show hospitality to strangers, for thereby
> some have entertained angels unawares. (Heb. 13:2)

Recognize Jesus in Every Stranger

Glancing at a stranger in a coffee shop should make us curious.
Who is she? What is she like? What does she believe about
God? We must strive to see past her appearance and pray for
compassion. She may look different from people we're used to
associating with, but in our hearts we can still love her. If we can
look at a stranger with love, we are welcoming her with the love
of God.

> For I was hungry and you gave me food, I was thirsty and
> you gave me drink, I was a stranger and you welcomed me.
> (Matt. 25:35)

Why Should We Be Hospitable?

Hospitality should come to us naturally because we are loved
by Jesus. If we have been saved from sin, death is no longer
our home. Our home is Jesus. He gave us life, food, shelter,
hope. Our foundation is that we love because He first loved us
(1 John 4:19). He is the ultimate host, giving us abundant life. As
we stand on this beautiful truth, we can be hospitable and loving
to others, compelled by His grace that we then extend to people
around us. To understand hospitality, we must understand the
gospel of Jesus, who reached into human history and gave us life,
by His death. Because we are loved, we have a "home" to share.
The most beautiful treasure that we can share is Jesus.

God Is Hospitable

Rescuing and redeeming us with His deep love, God is the most
hospitable of all. The gift of Jesus is the most hospitable gift in
history, and we are made alive through it daily. Made to reflect His
love, we reach out to others, inviting them to see God as He is.

It's Evangelistic

When we extend ourselves to meet the needs of others, we are saying something about the God we serve. Are we quick to tell why we are hospitable? Are we proud of God and His hospitality toward us? If we share our homes, we also share our hearts and the reason for the love we extend.

It Shows Acceptance

> In hospitality, the stranger is welcomed into a safe, personal, and comfortable place, a place of respect and acceptance and friendship.—Christine Pohl[1]

WHERE ARE WE TO BE HOSPITABLE?

We are to be hospitable anywhere we are: our homes, churches, workplaces, the coffee shop, or markets. We can invite people over to our homes and feed them, give them a place to sleep, meet their needs in prayer, or just listen. We can take a meal to someone who is struggling financially or who just lost a family member. Or, we can call someone on the phone to encourage them.

As I write this from my neighborhood coffee shop, I am reflecting on the conversation I just had with a lady next to me. I started talking with her and enjoyed getting to know how, in her sixties, she is struggling to find work. She opened up to me, a stranger, about her struggles and allowed me to see her need. Warmly, I responded and asked further questions, leaving her reflective and thankful to have chatted. God gave me an opportunity to be hospitable to this woman. I didn't have her in my home, but I invited her heart to be shared. Hospitality is when we provide for the needs of others by giving of ourselves—even something as simple as our attention in a warm conversation.

---

1   Pohl, Christine. *Making Room* (Grand Rapids, MI: Wm. B. Eerdmans Publishing, 1999), p. 13.

HOSPITALITY VERSUS ENTERTAINING

Often when we talk about hospitality, we think of "entertaining." As we prepare our homes for hosting a dinner, we also can prepare our hearts to serve those who enter. Hospitality does not try to impress, but to serve.

> Entertaining has little to do with real hospitality. Secular entertaining is a terrible bondage. Its source is human pride. Demanding perfection, fostering the urge to impress, it is a rigorous taskmaster that enslaves. In contrast, scriptural hospitality is a freedom that liberates. Entertaining says, "I want to impress you with my beautiful home, my clever decorating, my gourmet cooking." Hospitality, however, seeks to minister. It says, "This home is not mine. It is truly a gift from my Master. I am His servant, and I use it as He desires." Hospitality does not try to impress but to serve. —Karen Mains[2]

How do you know if you are being hospitable or just entertaining?

Entertaining	Hospitality
I want to look good	I want Jesus to look good
Emphasis on food or outer appearance	Emphasis on the hearts of those in your home
Preoccupied or apologetic about messes	Humbled by the mess and can still serve
Goal: To impress	Goal: To serve

WHEN IS HOSPITALITY WORSHIPFUL?

Remember Mary and Martha? Mary's hospitality was serving Jesus through her attentive heart. Martha's hospitality (albeit shrouded in grumbling and frustration) was serving Jesus

---

2   Mains, Karen. *Open Heart, Open Home* (Mainstay Church Resources, 1976), p. 28.

in action. Both kinds of activity are hospitable and can be worshipful, as long as your emphasis is on the hearts of those in your home. Martha could've been active in the kitchen and still had a heart joyfully focused on her Lord, working as an act of worship.

Hospitality is worshipful when your actions or attention communicate God's care for those in your home. Being sensitive to people's needs and serving them as they are among you helps people understand God's attentive affection for His children.

Hospitality as Worship
Hospitality takes the form of worship:

- When you want to serve others, making Jesus look good, not you. This doesn't require expensive meals and immaculately clean living rooms. If you have given your attention to the heart(s) of those in your presence, seeking to serve them by meeting their basic or special needs, you have considered them above yourself.

- When your demeanor is meek, humbled, and kind—desiring to love someone in your care.

- When you are willing to abandon a goal, flexible to attend to the need that is in front of you.

- When you desire to bless someone because of the love and grace Jesus constantly extends to you.

REFLECTION QUESTIONS

1. Are you friendly to strangers?

2. Do you look for opportunity for unexpected conversations?

3. What is your inclination when having people over to your home: entertaining or hospitality?

4. When does the fear of what others think of your home keep you from humble service or from inviting others into your life or heart?

5. Does your personal budget reflect biblical hospitality? Do you have a financial plan in place to be generous with what you have been given?

6. How is God inviting you into joyful, worshipful, biblical hospitality?

CHAPTER 26

Productive Planning

The plans of the diligent lead surely to abundance,
but everyone who is hasty comes only to poverty.

(Prov. 21:5)

Time is not *ours*. Time is God's. He created and rules over it. Our relationship with time is often harried, rebellious, or we ignore the clock altogether. Do you keep lists, schedules, plans? Do you execute them?

David Allen, of the popular book and productivity system *Getting Things Done,* says you can't manage time, but you can manage actions.[1] Before you manage actions though, you need to know what actions are yours to take. *Which* actions, and *what* is the level of priority for your actions?

The Master (God) gave us work to do and a certain amount of time to do it in. Stewarding our corner of His world and caring for people with diligence and wisdom requires us to be prayerful and purposeful.

While this chapter is about "practical planning," we have got to remember that the only true and lasting peace we can have while we work is knowing Jesus. Furthermore, it is His peace

---

1   Allen, David. *Getting Things Done* (New York, NY: Penguin, 2001).

that invigorates us to have purpose or meaning in our plans. Our plans can flow from our prayers.

We start with *prayer*, acknowledging why we plan—to worship God. Then, we respond to God with *purpose*, which evolves into a *plan*. Planning is the practical overflow of a heart that seeks to worship God in work. It is purposeful, because as God invites us to worship, our hearts can respond with action.

PRAYER—PURPOSE—PLAN

As we *pray*, desiring to worship Jesus, His grace enables *purpose*. And practically, purpose becomes a *plan*. To be purposeful in our stewardship, we must plan. As I wrote before in Chapter 17, "Prayer Brings Peace," planning can bring a quick relief to the chaos of our lives for a little while, but if we want peace amidst that chaos, prayer is priority number one. As we pray, we acknowledge God's right to the details, the schedules, and our plans. In prayer, we give the agenda to Him, and He gives us wisdom, directing us. So, what I am recommending is meek (aware of need) and confident (aware of His grace) planning.

What follows are practical steps for the "Prayer-Purpose-Plan" approach.

1. Schedule

The key is not to prioritize what is on your schedule, but to schedule your priorities. What are your priorities? Have you written them down? Have you and your spouse talked about what is essential to the vision and mission of your family? Start with a conversation about what is important for your time. Keep your lists in the same place: a file, a drawer, your computer, or an envelope. Write a to-do list, putting the most important tasks at the top. Keep a schedule of your daily activities to minimize conflicts and last-minute rushes.

Incorporate your lists into a schedule. Buy a week-at-a-glance appointment book, use a computerized calendar, or buy a business table-top calendar for your desk or wall. Write everything you need to accomplish in the calendar. Differentiate between the urgent and the vitally important.

The daily, weekly, and monthly plan should be posted in some form: a calendar on the inside of your cabinet door, on the fridge, or in a computer program, for those who are online often. Look at it frequently, as a reminder of what to prioritize. I have a calendar on the inside of a cabinet door in my kitchen that has our menu plan and social calendar showing guests, visits, play dates, appointments. This is not my household management calendar. I use my computer for household chores, birthday reminders, project lists, shopping lists, and the activities and events that are months away.

Synchronize your calendar and plans weekly with your spouse (if married) and/or children (if they are older and living in your home).

2. Prioritize Your Tasks
Time-consuming but relatively unimportant tasks can absorb a lot of your day. Prioritizing tasks will ensure you spend your time and energy on those that are truly important to you—and God. If the important ones aren't done, they create stress. Being thoughtful and prayerful about planning gives you a little more freedom to respond to urgent things.

3. Free Your Brain From "Open Loops"
In *Getting Things Done*, David Allen talks about "Open Loops." These are the items that swirl around in your brain and cause you to lie awake at night thinking about things like: what you should do tomorrow, the presents you need to buy, recipe ingredients for dinner, a conversation to have, hopes, regrets… random thoughts that need to be captured somewhere. Open loops can make us daydreamers or even lose sleep. Busy brains can rest if we prayerfully put most of those swirling thoughts to bed in a plan, list, or prayer. As soon as you realize you are out of peanut butter, put peanut butter on your grocery list, or as you accept a party invite, put the present on a list and the event on

the calendar. Otherwise, trying to remember all of it will take up brain space. Those "open loops" will start to diminish as we write things down.

4. Establish Routines

What is your morning routine? What do you try to accomplish before 9:00 a.m.? What is your routine while kids are napping? While getting your family out the door for an activity? Before going to bed? Establishing routines makes it easier for you to habitually accomplish what you need to do to run your home well.

5. Break Large, Time-Consuming Tasks into Smaller Tasks

Work on big tasks, a few minutes at a time, until you get them all done. Get an inexpensive timer, set it for 15 minutes, and challenge yourself to clean and organize one room, top to bottom. Maybe it is the competitiveness in me, but I love this! I do this with my kids as we tackle a room, having fun working together.

6. Limit Distractions

Block out time on your calendar for big projects. Try to focus on one thing. During that time, silence your phone and have self-control to not check email. You will have distractions if you have young children around or are in a work environment with intermittent knocks at your door. That is okay; don't be angry. Lovingly respond to "people distractions"; they aren't robbing you. Then after the conversation is over, get back to your planned task or project.

7. Keep an "Inbox" on Every Floor of Your House

My mother always said, "Make your trips count." The basic idea is that if you are going from room to room, take something with you. Having an inbox, bucket, or container that holds various miscellaneous items that go to other rooms can be an important time-saver. My kids are continually taking things from other rooms and leaving trails. It is helpful to throw those items in the container or basket when cleaning up. That way, clutter doesn't pile up and you can "make your trips count." You don't have to be neurotic about it, but you will see how many miscellaneous items pile up, and then you or one of your kids can empty the inbox in just a few minutes. Some ideas are to keep a bag in the car for items that go to the house, a container on the stairs, or a laundry basket for bedroom items.

8. *Get Plenty of Sleep, Enjoy a Healthy Diet, and Exercise Regularly*

Healthy choices can improve your focus and concentration, which will help improve your efficiency and complete your work in less time. Waking up early gives us opportunity to work out, study the Bible, take a brisk walk, get a few minutes to think about your day with your calendar, or pray that your heart would serve and love those near you and that you would depend on God to give you the courage, endurance, joy, and strength to accomplish what you need to do that day.

And....

9. *When in Doubt About How You Spend Your Time: Journal Your Productivity*

Keep track of your time by fifteen-minute increments for two weeks to see how you actually spend it. Compare this to what you've prayed about spending your time on. It will give you the motivation to make needed changes. This is helpful if you feel frustrated with not getting things done even though you feel like you are constantly working. You may find you are working frantically, but not necessarily working wisely.

God is patient with us as we learn and consider how to worship in work. These practical tips for organizing your work are meant to help. I pray Jesus will show us His grace continually when we work as a reflection of His love, and that our hands would merely express our gratitude by loving Him and those in our lives. Work is worshipful when we consider our hearts before an awesome God and respond with joy, repentance, and surrender!

Reflection Questions

1. Do you tend to leave out Prayer, Purpose, or Plan when coming up with to-do lists or a schedule?

2. What resonated most with you about how you spend your time each day as you read this chapter? Which tip seems most useful and accessible to you?

3. If you aren't already doing one (or any) of the nine practical strategies listed above, try one a week, adding the others with each succeeding week. As you progress, do you notice anything different about how you view time and productivity?

PART SIX:

Worship is All About Jesus

CHAPTER 27

Getting and Giving Grace

But by the grace of God I am what I am, and his grace toward me was not in vain. On the contrary, I worked harder than any of them, though it was not I, but the grace of God that is with me.

(1 Cor. 15:10)

WE CAN'T EVEN TAKE A BREATH WITHOUT GOD'S GRACE
It was about five years ago when the Holy Spirit urged me to write this book. I was convicted of my sinful independence and self-righteous work ethic. Heartbroken and repentant, I received radical cleansing grace from God, who forgave me of my sin. God continues to expose sin, but, at the same time, He expands my vision for worship. Redemption has been slow and beautiful. Ten steps forward and five steps back, all the way looking toward Jesus who is changing me. He is turning my heart's affections toward Himself—dramatically.

As I prayed through how to wrap up this book, I knew I needed to press the point about grace, lest you who are reading feel empowered by anything else. As God prompts us, we move forward, humbled by our need for Him. Every step, we know God's grace is moving us toward worshiping Him. We have no power within ourselves to muster up worship. It is all His grace at work.

HE WORKS, SO WE WORK

> And God is able to make all grace abound to you, so that having all sufficiency in all things at all times, you may abound in every good work. (2 Cor. 9:8)

As you work, picture God's grace filling you up with super-strength meekness and joy as you diligently labor. His grace abundantly provides. His grace faithfully fills you with love to accomplish the work He called you to.

Acknowledge His grace. We need it. Humbled, we can receive grace, as an act of worship. Knowing we can't do any action or think any good thought apart from His grace, we accept this good gift. Grace enables us to love—to reflect Jesus.

> Let us then with confidence draw near to the throne of grace, that we may receive mercy and find grace to help in time of need. (Heb. 4:16)

DON'T LOVE YOURSELF, LOVE GOD, GRATEFUL FOR GRACE

Often, as we become more self-aware, we become more aware of our inabilities. We see that we are frail humans. Exposed and uncomfortable with ourselves, we look for a remedy to this newfound awareness. Sometimes, we see this as an opportunity for God to rescue us in our need and embrace more of who we are in Christ: accepted, loved, adopted, redeemed. Other times, we look in the mirror and choose to buy into society's recommended remedy— self-love. If we could just love ourselves better, we would be confident, strong, and victorious. This isn't helpful advice. Loving ourselves more distracts us away from the only true help, the only lasting satisfaction—Jesus. Loving ourselves keeps our eyes off Jesus. We are more loved by God than we could ever imagine. As God helps us see both more of who *He is* and who *we are,* we can love Him more and ourselves less.

Yet, He sees us and He loves us, even in our sin. Instead of covering up our sin with happy thoughts about ourselves, we can honestly struggle in front of the mirror. The solution for sin isn't to love ourselves, it is to love Jesus. As love increases, our disdain for sin increases.

> And he said to him, "You shall love the Lord your God with all your heart and with all your soul and with all your mind. This is the great and first commandment. And a second is like it: You shall love your neighbor as yourself." (Matt. 22:37-39)

Jesus said, "Love your neighbor as yourself." Some have suggested that the "love yourself" part is assumed. The lack of loving ourselves isn't the reason for our unhappiness. Culture-makers enjoy providing false answers for our sin problem: low self-esteem, genetic pre-dispositions to addictions, depression, and/or environmental effects. We have to blame it on something, right?

We know the problem is sin. Below is a refresher on the broadness of our sin.

It is sin when:

"It is the glory of God not honored.

The holiness of God not reverenced.

The greatness of God not admired.

The power of God not praised.

The truth of God not sought.

The wisdom of God not esteemed.

The beauty of God not treasured.

The goodness of God not savored.

The faithfulness of God not trusted.

The commandments of God not obeyed.

The justice of God not respected.

The wrath of God not feared.

The grace of God not cherished.

The presence of God not prized.

The person of God not loved.

That is sin." —John Piper[1]

OUR SIN MAKES US UNGODLY

My days are filled with reminders of how ungodly I am. Sundays are usually pretty rough for me. My husband is a pastor, which means he is gone 14+ hours every Sunday. I believe there is some spiritual element to my Sunday Struggle, but for the most part, it is my sin that I wrestle, not my circumstances. The kids are especially lazy, whiny, and extra difficult. My house is a disaster because I took a small break from keeping it going the day before. I look around; chaos greets me. My heart's battle over sin is to respond to my children and home with gentleness as I seek to reclaim order in the house. Though Sunday is especially challenging, I struggle with this every day. I desire to be meek, embracing weakness, humbly, cheerfully managing my family and home—as an act of worship.

Often, though, I get cold and dutiful as I work through each room. If a child interrupts or adds more work, the tension swells in my heart. Suppressing the anger, I keep working. Working fast, with a cold heart. Sometimes, frustrated by how long it takes to do the easiest task while maintaining conversation with one or all of my children, I give them less than all of my attention or heart. Other times, I might not show my sin behaviorally, but the war still rages inside of me. I want order, but not at the expense of my family's peace. My recurring Sunday battle is *reclaim the house but still love my children well*. The challenges of this process reveal my desperate weakness and my deep need for God's grace. Grace enables me to fight and win the battle against my sin. And,

---

1   Piper, John. "The Greatest Thing in the World: An Overview of Romans 1-7" (September 2, 2001) http://www.desiringgod.org/resource-library/sermons/the-greatest-thing-in-the-world-an-overview-of-romans-1-7.

sometimes, loving the children means I don't reclaim my "clean" house.

> For while we were still weak, at the right time Christ died for the ungodly. For one will scarcely die for a righteous person—though perhaps for a good person one would dare even to die—but God shows his love for us in that while we were still sinners, Christ died for us. (Rom. 5:6-8)

As sinners, we are constantly made aware of our need for grace. He saves us. It is a gift.

> For by grace you have been saved through faith. And this is not your own doing; it is the gift of God. (Eph. 2:8)

Grace lights a fire in us that can't be put out. Our lives are lit up, showcasing God's glory. The more we realize the depth of grace extended, the deeper the worship. With humbled, radiant hearts—we worship.

WE ARE FORGIVEN

We can lay our sin at the foot of the cross. I can hand over my Sunday Struggle and know that God forgives my anger. God sent His son to pay the price I could never pay for my sin. He paid my debt in full and I rejoice. What amazing love Jesus has for us! He forgave us, forgives us, and will forgive our future sin.

As believers, we gratefully accept this beautiful gift of grace and suit up for life-long war. Battling the enemy and our sin, we look forward to true peace when the war is over. Even on seemingly peaceful days, I know deep down I've never known true, sinless peace. Jesus already won the war, but we will fight sin until we meet Him face-to-face.

My daily battles keep me mindful of His grace because He loves me. He loves you. God's love is deeply powerful and unceasing. His steadfast love never leaves us, no matter how hard we try to deny it. Our sin is never so great that God would leave us or stop loving us. Grace is given every second. God's fatherly affection is constant and personal to us.

> The steadfast love of the LORD never ceases;
> his mercies never come to an end;
> they are new every morning;
> great is your faithfulness. (Lam. 3:22-23).

Furthermore, when we recognize this abundant grace in our lives, we get to respond in gratitude by extending it to others.

WE FORGIVE OTHERS

> God's grace and forgiveness, while free to the recipient, are always costly for the giver.... From the earliest parts of the Bible, it was understood that God could not forgive without sacrifice. No one who is seriously wronged can "just forgive" the perpetrator.... But when you forgive, that means you absorb the loss and the debt. You bear it yourself. All forgiveness, then, is costly.—Tim Keller[2]

We can't pay the debt of our own sin, nor can we pay for the sin of others. Accepting God's grace and forgiveness for our own sin moves us to give forgiveness and grace to others freely, as an act of worship.

Forgiveness is worship because it is a heart response to the grace we have been given. The more we recognize how deeply we have been forgiven by God, the more we want to forgive others. Our forgiveness and love for others are inextricably tied to the love and forgiveness we experience because of Jesus.

> Therefore I tell you, her sins, which are many, are forgiven— for she loved much. But he who is forgiven little, loves little. (Luke 7:47)

---

2   Keller, Tim. *Counterfeit Gods* (New York, NY: Penguin, 2009), p. 89.

WORSHIP IS ALL ABOUT JESUS

As work becomes more worshipful in our lives, we are changed. With soft hearts, we become meek and steward our lives for the Master. Work becomes passionate when we see God's intentional love for us in the details. Repentant and tender, we labor—we worship. God moves our hands and our hearts and we worship Him.

REFLECTION QUESTIONS

1. When are you most aware of God's grace in your life?

2. When do you feel you most need God's grace?

3. When do you have tendencies to not extend His grace to others?

4. Are you aware of areas in your heart where you reject His grace?

Chapter 28

Invitation to Worship

We are saved to worship God. All that Christ has done in the past and all that He is doing now leads to this one end.

A.W. Tozer[1]

As this book comes to a close, I pray you are inspired to worship Jesus in your work. Living lives that glorify God in the mundane requires taking an intentional look at your heart, which I hope has happened for you. We have looked biblically at what it means to live a gospel-shaped life; to live lives that reflect God's grace. In our words, deeds, and most importantly our hearts—we desire to worship.

Do you see Jesus loving you as you do your laundry? When you work around the house or carpool yet another time, are you mindful of God? Are you becoming quicker at claiming the affection He so generously offers as you work? When you work through your daily task list, are you prayerful? How about your demeanor: are you tender-hearted and humbled by your weakness? And in that meek posture, are you grateful for God's grace?

---

1   Tozer, A.W. *Whatever Happened to Worship* (Camp Hill, PN: Wingspread Publishers, 2012), p. 94.

Can you believe God so lovingly and personally equipped you for your job? Take a moment and ponder how loved you are. Your Father reached into your life and heart to give you strength, joy, and His Holy Spirit to guide you as you grow in your worship. He guides your hands and heart every day, in each moment. His affection for you is constant.

> ...but the LORD takes pleasure in those who fear him, in those who hope in his steadfast love. (Ps. 147:11)

WORK AS WORSHIP

When asked in an interview about work as worship, J.I. Packer responded, "Worship is honoring God in any way and when one's labor is labor that one feels called to so that one is fulfilling one's vocation as one pursues it. Then it is a matter of conscious deliberate prayer, 'Lord, I offer you this, make what you can of it. I am doing it the best way I can to serve you and to honor you. Help me to do it as well as I am capable of doing it and make it a blessing to other people.'"[2]

When we seek to honor God in our work, we acknowledge His power and dominion over all creation as we steward what He has entrusted us with.

> Worship is the submission of all our nature to God. It is the quickening of conscience by His holiness; the nourishment of mind with His truth; the purifying of imagination by His Beauty; the opening of the heart to His love; the surrender of will to His purpose—and all of this gathered up in adoration, the most selfless emotion of which our nature is capable and therefore the chief remedy for that self-centeredness which is our original sin and the source of all actual sin.—William Temple[3]

---

2   Packer, J.I. "The Laity Lodge Interview," February 8, 2008, YouTube, http://www.youtube.com/watch?v=UpIYjFfaf1Y, retrieved December 9, 2012.

3   Temple, William. *Readings in St. John's Gospel,* First Series(London, Macmillan, 1939), 68.

Mindful of God

When we go about our day, it is easy to get mentally distracted. Worship is a *whole person* experience: the body and soul. Our whole person is designed for worship. If our body is working hard, we can engage emotionally and mentally with what we are physically doing. If our emotions are engaged, we tend to express it physically with tears, loud voice, or a smile.

Pray as you work that your heart would engage with your actions and your mind would click into thoughts of God. When I am overwhelmed in my work, this is easier. When I feel competent, I am less inclined to be mindful of Him. Pray for mindfulness.

Satisfied in God

> I will bless the LORD at all times;
> his praise shall continually be in my mouth.
> My soul makes its boast in the LORD;
> let the humble hear and be glad.
> Oh, magnify the LORD with me,
> and let us exalt his name together! (Ps. 34:1-3)

Are you restless as you work? At the end of the day, do you feel satisfied? Does it feel like you never get it all done? If so, are you going to the right place for that satisfaction? Does productivity truly bring peace?

True satisfaction is found in God. Being loved and known by Him are enough for us to find deep meaning and joy. We can rest satisfied because of God. "God is most glorified in us when we are most satisfied in him."[4]

Acknowledge His Presence

> You make known to me the path of life;
> in your presence there is fullness of joy;
> at your right hand are pleasures forevermore. (Ps. 16:11)

---

4   Piper, John. *Desiring God* (Colorado Springs, CO: Multnomah Books, 1986), p. 10.

As you become more deeply aware of your need for God in your daily work, you can stand firm in the truth that He is with you. He has given you His Spirit to guide, comfort, and protect your heart as you worship.

WHAT WORK AS WORSHIP ISN'T

Willpower: a horizontal relationship between me and some action; mustering up courage to accomplish something by my own drive.

Exercise tends to highlight willpower in my life. If I am to do any sort of exercise, I have to wake up at 5:30 in the morning. When my alarm goes off, I begin fighting between the two desires: sleep or exercise. Willpower would be to clench my teeth and resist the urge to press snooze and not get up. Willpower is reaching down deep to some super strength and fighting for what I want.

Willpower isn't disciplined worship. Willpower is about my strength. Worship is about God's strength.

That same alarm sound can blast me out of sleep-land, and my heart can submit in discipline to rise for exercise. The sweet surrender that submits desires and inspires action is worship. Waking up to work out is worshipful when my heart is engaged in what I believe God wants me to do, and with discipline, do it.

Worship: a vertical relationship between me and God; denying self and enjoying Christ's accomplishment. Worship is God-focused.

> Worship is an active response to the character, words and actions of God, initiated by His revelation and enabled by His redemption, whereby the mind is transformed (e.g. belief, repentance), the heart is renewed (e.g. love, trust), and actions are surrendered (e.g. obedience, service), all in accordance with His will and in order to declare His infinite worthiness.[5]

---

5   "Worship," Theopedia, http://www.theopedia.com/Worship#note-0, retrieved December 9, 2012.

God doesn't invite us to numb strength; he invites us to worship instead of to willpower.

> If the essence of worship is satisfaction in God, then worship can't be a means to anything else.—John Piper[6]

LIVING A WORSHIPFUL LIFE

Repentance

As we work and worship, our hands work busily as our hearts are mindful of Jesus. We don't do this perfectly, ever. As we struggle against sin, we repent. Repenting of our arrogance and sluggardly hearts and behavior, we know we deserve death. Repentance is seeing what our sin cost Jesus. We bow to our God, knowing He paid the price for sin. His death was truly in our place. And with every day and every sin, we are reminded of this death.

I still whine and complain like our sister, Martha, that my work doesn't go as expected. God gently nudges me to repent. The battle against pursuing my agenda instead of God's still rages. I easily forget His goodness. I still choose productivity above worship. God's grace invites my repentance. My sin is not too great for Him.

Sanctification (Dying to Sin and Living to Righteousness)

Forgiven! Washed clean! Loved! Jesus' death in our place! We are being changed. He is pursuing our hearts and getting glory from our joy in Him. As He changes us, our desires become sanctified. We continue to die to sin and live for Jesus. What a beautiful gift! We are being renewed each day.

> He himself bore our sins in his body on the tree, that we might die to sin and live to righteousness. By his wounds you have been healed. (1 Pet. 2:24)

---

6   Piper, John. "Gravity and Gladness on Sunday Morning, Part 1," Desiring God, September 12, 2008, http://www.desiringgod.org/resource-library/seminars/gravity-and-gladness-on-sunday-morning-part-1, retrieved on December 9, 2012.

Resurrection—Redemption

As my five year old sings, "My God is not dead, he is surely alive,"[7] I think about our hope in the resurrection. Such profound hope we have! Our God sits on a throne, ruling and reigning, and yet He knows us personally. He is attentive to His children, loving us every step of the way.

Because our God is alive, we can boast in His power to heal, forgive, and love us constantly! He has promised to redeem us from all suffering and sin. Sisters, we are loved, pure, and made new in Christ. Our work is redemptive as we live for Jesus, not our own glory. Instead of climbing career ladders, we cling to Jesus. We don't work for love, Jesus' work was enough. Because God's work is perfect, we don't put our identity in our job review.

Work As Evangelism

Living a cross-shaped life is having a passionate desire to see Jesus glorified. You don't have to be a famous evangelist to share the gospel. Remember, especially in your meekness, Christ is made great. Simply worshiping Jesus in what He has called and equipped you to do communicates the gospel, making Jesus look good, not you.

Work as worship will ultimately preach a message of God's love. Loving God and people will certainly put His grace on exhibit. Fearing the Lord in your heart, knowing His power is constant and His Spirit is at work in you, mean your work will be a sermon. As Christians, our lives are on constant display, and we never know exactly who is watching or when their curiosity about Jesus will be stirred.

> Likewise, wives, be subject to your own husbands, so that even if some do not obey the word, they may be won without a word by the conduct of their wives, when they see your respectful and pure conduct. (1 Pet. 3:1-2)

Our conduct in our labor has the power to move the hearts of people. Have you thought about who is watching you work?

---

7   Newsboys, "God's Not Dead (Like a Lion)," *God's Not Dead*, Inpop, 2011.

What questions about Jesus are forming in their minds? What does our work say about Jesus?

CONCLUDING THOUGHTS

What do you want your life to be about? If someone wrote an article about you, describing your passions, pursuits, and what brings meaning to your life, what would it say?

Let's return to Martha, the original inspiration for this work and worship journey. If someone wrote about Martha solely based on the story we have of her in Luke 10, it would be a sad story of a tattle-taling sister, focused on her own agenda, not her Lord Jesus.

I like to imagine Martha learning her lesson, repenting, and worshiping Jesus in her work. Her story of redemption could paint a picture of a holy God reaching into her life and patiently confronting her sin of independent, glory-seeking, grumbling work. Because of Jesus' death in her place, she accepts and rejoices in forgiveness and starts understanding what it would look like to become meek, grateful, and confident in her stewardship. Her fear of the Lord interprets her actions, and her heart is full of joy as she works. While she still struggles against conflicting desires, she knows her Jesus loves her, that her work doesn't define her— He does. Jesus is her reward.

Her work was worship. Is yours?

REFLECTION QUESTIONS

1. Have you started worshiping in your work? Have you experienced a difference in how you engage with work because of it?

2. Who are the people around you that see your attitude as you work? How can you glorify God without saying a word?

3. Are you more thankful for the work God has given you knowing that He was the one who imparted it to you?

THE
ENVY
OF Eve

FINDING CONTENTMENT IN
A COVETOUS WORLD

MELISSA B. KRUGER

paperback ISBN 978-1-84550-775-6
epub ISBN 978-1-84550-944-6
Mobi ISBN 978-1-84550-945-3

The Envy of Eve
Finding Contentment in a Covetous World

MELISSA B. KRUGER

What's truly at the heart of our desires? *The Envy of Eve* guides readers to understand how desires grow into covetousness and what happens when this sin takes power in our hearts. Covetousness chokes out the fruit of the Spirit in our lives, allowing discontentment to bloom. The key to overcoming is to get to the root of our problem: unbelief – a mistrust of God's sovereignty and goodness. An ideal resource for deeper study or group discussion.

I commend this fine book ... with a prayer that we all read and follow her Biblical counsel to fully understand the condition we are in and flee quickly to the One who truly satisfies our deepest longings and our true desires.

Michael Milton
Chancellor and Chief Executive Officer, The James M. Baird,
Jr. Chair of Pastoral Theology, Reformed Theological Seminary,
Charlotte, North Carolina

With empathy and grounded biblical insight, Melissa Kruger shows us the path to abiding joy amidst life's varied 'ups' and 'downs'.

Lydia Brownback
Author of *Contentment*, Wheaton, Illinois

In an age and culture where we all tend to have an overdeveloped sense of entitlement, this book makes a brilliant diagnosis that goes right to the heart of the problem.

Ann Benton
Author and family conference speaker, Guildford, England

With I've-been-there understanding and been-in-the-Word insight, Melissa B. Kruger helps us to look beneath the surface of our discontent, exposing our covetous hearts to the healing light of God's Word.

Nancy Guthrie
author of *Seeing Jesus in the Old Testament* Bible Study Series

Christian Focus Publications

Our mission statement –

STAYING FAITHFUL
In dependence upon God we seek to impact the world through literature faithful to His infallible Word, the Bible. Our aim is to ensure that the Lord Jesus Christ is presented as the only hope to obtain forgiveness of sin, live a useful life and look forward to heaven with Him.

Our books are published in four imprints:

CHRISTIAN
FOCUS

Popular works including biographies, commentaries, basic doctrine and Christian living.

CHRISTIAN
HERITAGE

Books representing some of the best material from the rich heritage of the church.

MENTOR

Books written at a level suitable for Bible College and seminary students, pastors, and other serious readers. The imprint includes commentaries, doctrinal studies, examination of current issues and church history.

CF4•K

Children's books for quality Bible teaching and for all age groups: Sunday school curriculum, puzzle and activity books; personal and family devotional titles, biographies and inspirational stories – because you are never too young to know Jesus!

Christian Focus Publications Ltd,
Geanies House, Fearn, Ross-shire,
IV20 1TW, Scotland, United Kingdom.
www.christianfocus.com